D0681191

# The Journey

## by

## Lori Todaro

authorHOUSE™

1663 LIBERTY DRIVE, SUITE 200
BLOOMINGTON, INDIANA 47403
(800) 839-8640
WWW.AUTHORHOUSE.COM

No part of this book may be reproduced, stored in a retrieval system, or transmitted by any means without the written permission of the author.

First published by AuthorHouse 12/01/04

ISBN: 1-4208-1105-3 (sc)

Printed in the United States of America
Bloomington, Indiana

This book is printed on acid-free paper.

In honor of my Parents

To my Boys -Thanks for always bringing out the best in me!

To my Husband -Your strength has gotten us through. Your love is a gift.

Thank you!

As I close my eyes and picture my life, I see endless waters. Each obstacle, each accomplishment, each step along the journey, I compare to running waters. I feel exhilarated each time I prepare for the jump across the body of water and land safely on the other side.

For awhile, I had so much support on the rough waters. I had a

strong, dependable raft......My Dad!

I can recall the days after my Father's death so well. There was

so much chaos, so much raw emotion, and so much total disbelief

that he was gone. As far back as I can remember my dad was

the one who kept everything together. He was a character. The

way he laughed made others laugh. His jokes were so dumb they

were actually funny. No matter what bad thing was going on, he

somehow turned it into something good!

My parents raised me Catholic, although my dad claimed not

to have a "religion". What I observed on Thanksgiving Day in

1987 proved to the contrary. Walking into the dining room with a

homeless man, Dad yelled to my mom and asked her to set another

place. His compassion toward the man was a way he modeled his

faith. Later my mom asked my father, "What were you thinking?"

He simply said, "I was thinking I'd never want to be alone and

hungry and cold!" My father was a simple man, with a simple

plan!

I thank God for his presence in my life. The way he led his life

taught me many things. I learned to take chances. I learned

to be the real me no matter what others think. I also learned disappointment from his death, such as things don't always go your

way, life isn't always fair, and bad things happen to good people.

Sometimes we are unprepared for the bad times. As long as we live

each day to the fullest, there will be no regrets!

Another thing I learned from my dad's death is not to dwell on the

negatives, which is also about taking chances. Being married to a

police officer has also enforced this philosophy. A question I am

frequently asked when people hear of my husband's profession is

"Aren't you frightened?" I think, *frightened of what?* My husband

is trained at what he does. He loves his career, and he loves his

family. If I worried each day, I wouldn't really be living, now

would I? My dad went out on his boat, a week before his 50th

birthday. He was doing something he loved, on his own time, by

his own will. He never came home! I would be unhappy and scared

all the time if I wasted a single moment worrying over something

I cannot control. I look back on my dad's death as the beginning

of my adult life. Yes, I was already married and a mom, but I still

hadn't grown up! Experiences really develop who you are and who

you will become.

Daddy,

I have so much to say to you, and have no idea where to begin. You never prepared me for this. I thought I'd always be able to run to you when I didn't understand something. I thought for sure you'd be there to meet my children, to help me care for Mom, and to comfort me with your humor. When I felt hurt by someone or something I thought you'd be here to just put your arms around me like you always did. I am angry, I am sad, I feel scared. I want to thank you for adding so much to my life, though. I am grateful for all our wonderful memories. I am so glad that you met and loved Tony. I am so glad you were there when we welcomed Joey into the world. That is one of my favorite memories.

I remember everything. I've heard that over time you sometimes forget things about those who have died; I've heard that you create your own stories. I remember everything!

There is so much I learned from you. I learned to never judge others because you never know what the future holds. I've learned to take chances and enjoy life. I've learned that being a wife and a mother are two separate things. You were my dad, and you were Mom's husband, two very different roles. I've just learned that, though, since I am a mom and a wife. I wish you were here to know how much I understand now. I miss you terribly! You would get such a kick out of the boys. They are so cool. Joey has a heart of gold. He wears his heart on his sleeve and reminds me a lot of you. Vinny is so bright; he really makes me think. He is so curious, so full of life. You'd be intrigued by him. Nino is such a hero. He is so incredibly brave. His shyness worries me, though; I wish you were here to help comfort him. He is so funny too! He has a silly side of him that reminds me of you. He says weird things like" turnip head" and "watermelon butt", just like you! Angelo is a gift! He is becoming his own person each day, but he is truly a gift. He brought joy into our lives when we were overwhelmed with fear about Nino. He has a gentle spirit. He is so sweet and happy.

Looking back I have thought a great deal about my marriage in relation to your death. I think if Tony and I could handle the shock of your death together, nothing can destroy us. You'd be so proud of Tony; he tries so hard. He does his very best for the boys and me. He tells me that he learned so much from you. You'd be proud of the man he is; you'd be grateful for the father that he is.

All of these things I wish you were here to be a part of. I know that you are

never far from us, but in the physical sense I wish you were here.

I replay that night almost every day in my head. How did it happen Daddy?

Did you just trip like they said? How? You knew the boat so well. You

knew where the running lights were. What did you think as you were

falling? Did you think of me? Did you feel pain? Did you feel scared? I wish

I were there. I would have pulled you from that water and never let you go!

I wasn't there! I am so sorry that I wasn't there! I have wanted to say that

for so long, but say it to whom? You're gone! I pray that you didn't suffer.

You deserved so much more! Your 50th birthday party was going to be a

blast! I'd much rather have been at a party than at your funeral.

I have been trying for years to write a letter to you. It is coming up on the

11th anniversary of your death. I cannot believe it! The hurt and disbelief

are still as real today as it was then. Then there was just denial in the

equation. You know, we never got to see your body when it was pulled from

the water; someone else identified it. I felt robbed of that! However, it has

kept me going all these years. The autopsy report was incorrect, so all this

time whenever I get bummed I will say to Tony, "You know maybe my dad is on a remote island somewhere living like a King!" Well Dad you are; but the island is heaven, and you are royalty there!

I know I will see you again. In the meantime Dad, I want to make you proud. I want to take all the characteristics I learned from you and to be the best me that I can be. I love you, Dad; I always will. Each night before I go to sleep, I thank God for your gift in my life.

Love,

Lori

# Journal

*11/12/03*

*Dear Friends*

*Once again, many prayers were answered! We are home, and the surgery went well! Nino has been resting since we arrived home. His belly is a little upset from the anesthesia, and he is very tired. Tony and I are thrilled that he is tired, because the side effects from the medications he is currently taking are awful! He is totally wired. Lora invited Joe and Vinny over for the afternoon, and they couldn't be happier. Thanks, Lora! Our neighbor Pat sent a pot of vegetable soup over, Nino's favorite. He will be on a soft diet for 2-3 days, and may begin to eat what he can tolerate after that. The fridge is full of Jell-O and ice pops! No one in the house is complaining about the goodies, especially Tony!*

*Last night something wonderful happened and I'd like to share it with all of you. In the midst of chaos in our house, we just got home from hair cuts and flu shots, I was trying to make dinner, Angelo was covered in lollipop, and the other boys were just getting out of the tub and shower. The house was a MESS and guess where Tony was? He was on duty, of course. Well, the baby was in the tub and there is a knock at the door! It was a special friend of mine. Between chauffeuring her children to many activities, she* stopped by. Oh, I forgot to mention that I was also on the phone with one of

the doctors while all this is going on. Anyway, I apologized a million times

over for the appearance of the house (Those of you who know me, know it

drives me crazy when there is a mess), and she calmly helped me control the

chaos and gently handed me holy water from Lourdes! It was so awesome

to receive holy water from Lourdes, the one to whom I am offering special

prayers for Nino. That special friend knows who she is. Thank you! Last

evening another special friend invited me to Applebee's for dessert, knowing

I needed the break! I had a wonderful time. Thanks! Before the night was

over someone else that has become very dear to me offered me more holy

water from Lourdes; it touched my heart more than you will ever know.

There have been many SO many acts of kindness for our family; I cannot

thank everyone enough! I have one more thought on the subject of kindness

that I wanted to share with you. If you have ever been to a Todaro party of

any kind, you know how fabulous the cakes are that Mr. Kilmore and his

wife make! They went above and beyond for us recently. Thank you! Please

know how thankful we are to ALL of you!

Today was the beginning of the "one day at a time" journey with Nino.

Please continue to pray. Continue to look for emails. Continue to know how *blessed we feel. God is looking out for our family, and for all of you! Take*

*care of yourselves, and always be good to each other!*

*Fondly,*

*Tony and Lori*

*11/16/03*

*Dear Friends,*

*Hi to everyone. We all complained that it was too warm for the month of*

*October, now look at this weather. Warm weather, where are you? Just a*

*short message so that you know we are thinking of you and that we are so*

*grateful that so many of you care so much!*

*Friday morning Nino received an MMR vaccine and flu shot. Friday*

*evening he had some sort of reaction. We believe it wasn't necessarily from*

*the shots, just from a combination of what he has been through this week!*

*Last night was tough, but today was a little better. We made cookies and*

*pineapple upside down cake with my mom. The boys had a blast, and we*

*even managed to sneak in a Math lesson with measurements, and Science*

*talking about solids and liquids! Needless to say, flour was everywhere; but*

*these are moments to cherish! We spent a lot of time cuddling and reading* today. Sometimes, even if Nino is having a rough day, the cuddling makes it all okay. I wouldn't wish this on anyone! Our situation has opened our eyes to so many important things: our faith, our blessings, the boys, our family, and our friends. It really made us re-evaluate our priorities! I thank God every day for our children. I also thank him for giving us the strength to do what needs to be done. The other day a nurse said, "I bet you are questioning why God would do this!" God didn't do this. He is just right next to us, helping us get through it!

We hope you are all doing well. You are in our thoughts and prayers! Tomorrow is Sunday. Many of you will attend Mass, or Church, or Kingdom Hall, or any place you go to worship. When you leave, do one kind thing for someone else and think of Nino. As always, thank you and God bless.

Take care of yourselves and each other.

Fondly,

Tony and Lori


11/17/03

Dear Friends,

This will be short. I promise! Tony is saying, "Lori, those who know us, know that is NOT possible!" Anyway, we hope you are all well! How many of you completed your assignment for Sunday? When leaving your place of worship, did you do something kind for someone else? Imagine if we all did that once a day. What a world we would live in.

Nino has had a rough weekend. At first we thought it was a reaction to everything his little body went through this past week! Our thoughts are beginning to change. Our doctor from Hershey decided to try the Indocin again. He has had a fever ranging from 101-105 since Friday. His belly is really hurting; so, of course, he is not eating or drinking! His legs are a little sore, but he is getting around fine. Massage from Mom does the trick! Dr. Holly, our pediatrician and friend, thinks he needs to be seen tomorrow. This is not a regular "flare" (attack), so possibly there is something else going on. He is in the process of being weaned off the steroids he has been on since April, so this may actually be the "real" disease showing its true colors! We will know more tomorrow; we know we are in great hands, in GOD'S and in the wonderful doctors'! So, say a prayer for Nino! Okay?

We made it to noon Mass yesterday. Nino leaned on the pew the whole time because his legs hurt. I looked at him and thought, he's such a hero! He never *complains and loves going to Mass. He is our hero! How many of us are sore and achy and don't go to work or cancel plans?*

*One of the songs we sang at Mass was "Eye Has Not Seen". It is one of my favorites. I will bring this to a close by sharing some of that song with you, and how I apply it to our journey with Nino! "Eye has not seen, ear has not heard, what God has ready for those who love Him. Spirit of love, come give us the mind of Jesus, teach us the wisdom of God." God is guiding us each step of our way. We have to believe that! Who knows what God's plan is for each of us? We don't know! The Spirit of love will guide us to His wisdom. Trust in Him!*

*Goodnight for now. Take care of yourselves and each other!*

*Fondly,*

*Tony and Lori*

*Rob: Uh-oh! I heard about it the whole way home, and not just from Tony!*

*Denay and Brian: Thank you for helping last night.*

*Nina: The cookies are GONE. I did not even get one! Thanks for taking Rexx for a walk!*

*Holly: Thanks!*

# Journal

Andrea and Barry: The cards made both of us smile!

Polly: Thanks for the kind words.

Father Waltersheid: You have made a difference.

Robin: God placed us in each others lives. I thank Him daily!


11/20/03

Dear Friends,

Just wanted to say hello and keep you all informed. Your thoughts and prayers are amazing. We apologize for not returning all of your calls. The concern and care you have shown to our family is truly overwhelming! We really want to take this opportunity to thank you. Angie, the lasagna was terrific; Vinny had five servings! Today is Monday, and it was an okay day for Nino. The boys were able to get a lot of their school work done early in the day, so in the afternoon Nino rested. Father Waltersheid visited with us this evening and gave Nino a special blessing. He also gave each of us a prayer card. Did you know that Our Lady of Lourdes is to whom we should offer special prayers of healing? If you have ever been to Mount Saint Mary's in Maryland, the Grotto is gorgeous! That is what I picture when I pray to her for Nino. Tony asks Saint Christopher to help him stay strong. It *doesn't matter what your prayer may be, we just thank you one and all for including our family. Wednesday is quickly approaching, and I am a nervous wreck. The surgery will be first thing in the morning.*

*The boys will get their flu shots in the morning, and Tony and I will get ours on Friday. It is really just a precaution; while on chemotherapy, Nino's immune system is suppressed; and it is very easy, as well as very dangerous, to get the flu or any other virus. As a precaution, we are all getting STUCK! Ha-ha!*

*Well, it has been a busy day. I should bring this to a close for tonight. Please know again how much we appreciate ALL the kindness. Remember my last email? If you forgot to tell those around you how much they mean to you, do it NOW! Don't waste one minute of the time God has given you. Tony and I share a favorite quote that I'd like to share with you. WHO YOU ARE IS GOD'S GIFT TO YOU. WHAT YOU MAKE OF YOURSELF IS YOUR GIFT BACK TO GOD! Make yourself an instrument of peace, and love those around you! Take care of yourselves and each other.*

*Fondly,*

*Tony and Lori*

*P. S. On a lighter note, Tony received word today about his new position!*

*December 5th will be his last day at his current station. On December 8th, he*

*will officially begin his new assignment, YEAH!*

*PSS. Robin, the medal is beautiful!*


*11/22/03*

*Dear Friends,*

*Hope this finds you all well!*

*It is Saturday evening. The boys are settled, and the packing begins. We*

*have been waiting for this trip to National Institutes of Health (NIH) in*

*Bethesda, Maryland, for a long time. We were first told about Dr. Kastner,*

*a doctor at NIH, in April. Preparing for the trip and packing for the trip are*

*so different from being on our way. There are so many complex feelings that*

*are happening right now. Wouldn't it be wonderful if NIH's test results*

*lead the doctors to a treatment other than Methotrexate for*

*Nino's condition! We also don't want to get our hopes up now that we have*

*prepared ourselves for the journey ahead. We are actually going to leave on*

*Monday morning, so that we spend one less day away from the boys. When*

*we arrive, we will check into The Children's Inn where we will be staying.*

*We are then scheduled to meet with the nursing staff. Our appointment with Dr. Kastner is Tuesday morning at 6:45. If all goes well, we will be home Wednesday afternoon. If they decide to begin the medication at NIH, we will have to see how the medicine affects Nino. We pray we will be home in time to prepare a Thanksgiving meal with our boys.*

*As I type, I cry. I really need to share with you how this completely changes a FAMILY! You find strength you never knew you had. You cherish the moments your husband holds your hand for no reason. You listen to your children argue over the Game Boy, and take the time to interrupt and explain how NOT important that is! I worry about not being home to stuff the turkey on Wednesday evening, just as we do every year, just as I did every year with my mother and grandmother as far back as I can remember. I also trust that God has touched the boys' hearts; they have been so wonderful about "understanding" the situation. Many of you have offered to make meals, to help with the boys, etc… Thank you!*

*Usually I can go on forever. Tonight is a little difficult for me! My heart goes out to Tony. I have the ability to talk, and to express myself; he is quiet and private. He is hurting, and scared. Pray for him. I continue to pray to Our Lady of Lourdes. We pray the rosary each morning and bless ourselves* with the holy water from Maria and Pam! You are special ladies! Tonight, I

worry! I trust, but still worry.

We were at a friend's birthday party all afternoon, and watching Nino run

and play hide and seek tag made me so happy. Last week was rough for him!

I really just wanted to pretend all is normal. Unfortunately, that is not

the case. We will do what needs to be done. We will do it with faith. We

will do it with love for our family! Each day I pray that God will give me

STRENGTH to be a good MOM.

I don't think many of you will ever know how much you have touched our

lives with your kind words and deeds. In the chapel there is a note in a

child's handwriting that says, "Please pray for Joey Todaro's little brother,

Nino!" Many of you have mentioned it to me! I wanted to give that kid

a great big hug! That is what this journey is all about for us. Do unto

others. Reach out to others. Care about others. Apparently this child has a

wonderful example to follow.

I better bring this to a close and finish packing. Please know you are all in

our thoughts and prayers! We thank you for your kindness. When we return

and things are settled we will get a message out to all of you. As it stands,

we will return Wednesday afternoon.

# Journal

Next Wednesday, December 3rd, we are to arrive at Hershey at 7:00 AM for the first treatment.

We will do our best to keep you posted!

Peace be with all of you.

Fondly,

Tony and Lori



11/25/03

Hello to everyone!

It is Tuesday, a little before 5:00 PM; and we just got back to the Children's Inn after spending the whole day at the hospital. Nino and Tony are racing each other on Nintendo, and I thought I would share our day with you. It was a day of many tests for Nino! We arrived at the hospital at 7:15. We met with a wonderful team of doctors, as well as with Dr. Kastner. The man is brilliant! He spends his life studying these bizarre genetic disorders. We have another test to do in the morning, and we may head for home sometime in the afternoon. Thank you, GOD! I will stuff the turkey with my boys after all. God is good!

# Journal

After the testing process and consulting with the doctors, we have ALL decided there is another road to take. Once again, thank GOD! We entered Nino into a protocol (STUDY) which conducts studies on children with the same periodic fever symptoms. Maybe in time they will discover a "name" for this. Until then, we trust what the doctors already know!

There is a fairly new drug ENBREL which is what Nino will begin next Wednesday, December 3. It does cause suppression of the immune system so we will have to be careful about his exposure to infections. We were also told he may get "sicker" while on this medication from infections he may catch. It DOES NOT have the same side effects as the chemotherapy does! (Did I tell you that GOD is good?) It is an injection that we will give him twice weekly. The doctors at Hershey will teach us how to do everything on Wednesday. Another blessing, NIH takes care of the entire expense of the medications because Nino is part of this study! I told you God has something amazing planned for this little hero. Wouldn't it be wonderful if by his taking part in this protocol another child's illness is "named" because of what they already know about Nino! We will return every three months to NIH for routine checkups. In the meantime, we will have routine care with Carlisle Pediatric Associates and Hershey Medical Center. We are in great hands!

## Journal

*It is amazing here at NIH! The Children's Inn is beautiful! There are many families here with so many different stories to share! The kids are incredible! Your hearts would be touched. You would be humbled!*

*I do hope this finds you all well. We are in good spirits. We love NINO! We miss the boys terribly, but know that my mom is taking great care of them! Please remember my message to all of you. Be kind to each other; go above and beyond. You cannot imagine the difference it makes in people's lives! Our journey has begun. We are ready; we have faith and love and will never ever lose hope!*

*God bless all of you.*

*Fondly,*

*Tony, Lori and Nino*


*11/30/03*

*Dear Friends,*

*We hope this finds you all well and rested after the Thanksgiving holiday. We also pray many of you counted all of your blessings and then counted them again! Our turkey was delicious, much better than any turkey I can remember! We usually go around the table, oldest to youngest, and say* aloud the things for which we are most thankful. My mom cried tears

of thanksgiving the entire meal. I held it together until Tony shared his

thoughts about all of us being able to be together, including my mom, and

how thankful he was that Nino will receive the treatments that will help

him feel better. He then expressed his thanks to God about our family being

so strong.

We are doing okay. When we returned from NIH, Vinny had a sore throat

and fever. Angelo had a runny nose and cough. These things normally would

not be a big deal; but, needless to say, these are not usual circumstances. We

really have to shield Nino from "infections" while he's on Enbrel. Exposure

to common viruses can make him very sick, and exposure to live viruses

(chicken pox, TB, measles, etc.) can be dangerous. He is an energetic, curious,

5-year-old boy. It's going to be hard to "shelter him", but we have to keep

him as well as possible.

He was running a fever (103-105) all day Friday. Saturday morning he felt

good! He went to basketball practice and did a great job! Last evening he

complained about his belly hurting, and his legs were a little stiff. Today

Tony took Joe and Vinny for a hike. Nino really wanted to go, but we *decided against it! It is hard sometimes for him to understand, but long hikes*

*are sometimes difficult and much harder with the cold weather!*

*We want to thank you ALL again for your kind words and deeds. You have*

*touched our lives and hearts much more than you will ever know!*

*NIH was unbelievable! Unless you are there, you will never understand.*

*The families are amazing! There were so many sick children. Some were not*

*as sick as Nino; some were dying! It was a valuable life lesson for us to be*

*there and meet these families and know that we are not alone. Pray for these*

*families PLEASE.*

*The Children's Inn is just a big house. Families from all over the world stay*

*at no expense. It is run completely by donations. The people at NIH and at*

*the Children's Inn are angels in our lives. We will return about every three*

*months, and that is where we will stay. The only thing we need to provide is*

*food.*

*Wednesday will be our first treatment. We are a little nervous about giving*

*Nino injections ourselves, but Hershey will help us with everything on*

*Wednesday since it is our first time.*

# Journal

Nino will get the injections every Wednesday and Saturday, so Saturday we will be even MORE nervous! Please keep him in your thoughts! We will continue to keep you posted.

Did anyone read the article Andrea C wrote about our family in "The Patriot"? What an amazing friend she is! If you read her words, you probably cried. We did! We felt truly blessed that she shared our story and really got our message across.

If you have learned anything from our emails, I hope you understand how blessed we feel. This is a situation in our life. Nino is the most precious gift we could ever have received (Joe, Vinny and Angelo are too!). The gifts we are given, including material things, are never fully ours. Nothing is really ours. They are gifts with which we are blessed. They touch our lives for awhile and then move on. We now treasure our gifts differently than we did before our journey with Nino began. We look at things differently. We treasure each other more. We give thanks for the smallest of things knowing that the big things can be overwhelming! We hope that through this journey with us, you too come to share those same feelings!

We are going to bring this to a close. Who knows what today is? It is the first Sunday of Advent! As we were preparing our Advent wreath, we *talked with the boys about what preparation means! We feel our family has been preparing for our Nino journey for a long time. Is it possible for you to imagine the sacrifice God made for us? He sent His only Son into the world knowing what would happen. Mary knew the pain and suffering her Son would endure! We remember that, and never let that get too far from our thoughts. Welcome the Advent season into your lives and prepare yourselves and your families for the coming of the LORD!*

*Joy and Peace be yours!*

*Tony and Lori*

*A very special thank you to Andrea!*


*12/01/03*

*Dear Friends,*

*Good evening. ALL of the boys are asleep. Tony is on duty, and I thought I'd fill you in.*

*Yesterday was the BIG day. The emotions I experienced were unbelievable. I could not believe I was going to stick my baby with a needle. I am the mother who cries at the pediatrician's when the boys get their shots! (Right, Dr. Holly?) Well, we DID IT! It was okay. Nino is SO brave. I truly find* comfort in watching him "handle" everything. Last night, I prayed that God would always keep my heart humble! I asked HIM to never let me forget the feelings that I have felt over the last year on our journey. Our family's journey has profoundly changed my life. Yesterday was a day I will remember forever. It wasn't about sadness or pain. It was about life and living, and joy and triumph! Our doctor at Hershey told us yesterday that there are about fifty children that he sees as patients who have the same symptoms as Nino's symptoms. Because Nino was the "sickest", he was the one sent to NIH. That, my friends, is a blessing.

The medication alone costs $1200 a month, and insurances WILL NOT pay for it! Families are losing their homes just to keep their kids functioning. Because we are part of the study at NIH, all medication costs are COMPLETELY covered! These are the things we focus on! These are the things that make me truly thankful.

We didn't get home from Hershey until after 8:00 last evening. I had to go out to Wal-Mart at about 11:00. We needed supplies: Lysol wipes for the bathroom; kitchen antibacterial wipes; antibacterial hand lotion for the car; antibacterial soap; a container to store medications in the refrigerator; a container for the needles, gauze, etc.; and, of course, Veggie Tales band-aids.

*You get the picture! I cried throughout the store. People were looking at me kind of funny, as I was thinking if only they knew! I felt like we had just jumped across a river and landed on the other side. WE REALLY ARE ON OUR WAY! GOD is right there beside us, and we wouldn't have it any other way. Please take care of yourselves, and each other. Be there for others; take the extra step!*

*I have spoken to some of you in the last couple of days. Please don't be afraid to ask us questions if you have them. Also, don't be afraid of, or for, NINO. Believe the best and pray for him. Know that he is in good hands. Say a prayer for Tony and me on Saturday. That's the first time we will have to administer the shots ourselves! If any of you are nurses and are available Saturday afternoon to help with the injection, please let me know. Please keep in my mind that we would love to see you, but we need to be careful about exposing Nino to any infections. His immune system is suppressed and the littlest germ can make him ill!*

*I should bring this to a close for now. Please continue to look for our updates. We are very thankful so many of you care so much! I hope you are finding comfort in our updates. It comforts us to share our journey with you!*

# *Journal*

*Someone suggested that I make a journal for Nino with all of our updates.*

*That idea really touched my heart! I am a nut about writing letters and*

*stories for the boys! If anyone happens to have any of my emails saved and*

*can print them out and get them to us, it would be greatly appreciated!*

*Goodnight for now!*

*Fondly,*

*Lori*

*FYI, tomorrow is Tony's last day at his current station. He officially begins*

*his new position on Monday.*

*Jackie ~ The lollipops are all gone! I wish you could have seen Nino's face*

*when he came home from the hospital and the package was waiting for him*

*on the dining room table! Thank you, FRIEND!*

*Tracy ~ You will never know how much it meant!*

*Andrea ~ You really are a one-of-a-kind lady. Thank you for being in our life!*

*Mitzi ~ I think you are our guardian angel. Thanks for waiting and for*

*making me smile.*

*Dani ~ Thanks for taking Nino to the game room. You made his day!*

# Journal

12/11/03

Dear Friends,

We received amazing news today! Our friends at The Knights of Columbus have chosen to raise funds for a Therapeutic Jacuzzi for NINO! Haven't I told you how good GOD is? The Knights read Nino's story and are organizing everything! Here are the details and please spread the news! On Sunday, December 14, 2003, from 9:00 to 12:30, the Knights will sponsor a Breakfast with Santa. The all-you-can-eat breakfast includes eggs, pancakes, and other delicious foods. Santa will arrive at 9:30 and will have gifts for all of the children! Three savings bonds will be given away to three lucky children! Adults are $4.50-Children are $3.50-Children under 5 are free. There will also be a donation jar available. All proceeds will go toward the purchase of the Jacuzzi.

Usually the profits from the breakfasts are between $300 and $400. The Big Ugly Warehouse in York has offered us a wonderful deal: a price that is close to wholesale price, no delivery or set up fee, the cover at no extra cost, and chemicals for a year! They need a deposit of $400 before the end of the year! Then, we have 120 days to pay it off. The total is $3,970, which includes tax and everything! That is our goal!

# Journal

The Knights will hold a Boyd's Bear Bingo fundraiser on MARCH 28TH, which is when they hope to raise the remaining amount due. As soon as tickets go on sale, I will let you know! By the beginning of April, Nino will hopefully have his Jacuzzi. Praise God!

I do want to share with you what Nino said when I told him about our finally being able to get a Jacuzzi for him. He said, "At our house? Then my legs won't hurt anymore!"

We have been asking our insurance to help pay for this for over two years, so this is truly an amazing Christmas present. Do you see? Do unto others! Always reach out for someone else. We are so blessed and so touched by the kindness.

Please try to come out and have breakfast with Santa on Sunday!

God bless you all!

Peace and Love,

Tony and Lori


12/15/03

Good evening, everyone!

It is busy here tonight, but I just had to get a message out to everyone to share our great news! Despite the weather, the Santa breakfast went on as planned. There was a wonderful turn out. It is a great compliment to our family that so many of you care so much. You know that I always share the do unto others message? Well, kindness has been abundantly showered upon us during these last few months. Thank you one and all. The Knights of Columbus did the calculating and informed us today that the total contributed to the "Nino Fund" is $1,004! Have I not told all of you how good GOD is? He is right beside us on this journey.

Not having Nino's medical expenses covered by insurance can be so frustrating. I am on the phone, sometimes for hours at a time, battling the insurance company to pay for many medical expenses for Nino. Many times things are denied due to "lack of diagnosis". Insurance companies unfortunately are led by money and not compassion. They have told us more than once that they "cannot get personal"! What they fail to realize is that this is very personal! This is our five year old beautiful son who is seizing from a 107.0 fever, not walking due to the arthritis, or vomiting from the ulcers in his belly! THIS IS VERY PERSONAL! We never give up, we keep on fighting. We also never doubt or blame GOD through any of this. We just keep giving thanks, because there are so many people who are worse off than we are. How many of you know someone who has lost a child? We have ours to hold and cuddle each day. How many of you know someone who is working two or three jobs just to keep food on the table? How many of you wish you were able to "buy" more Christmas gifts, and forget about those families who will wake up in a cardboard box on Christmas morning? Thank you, God! Thank you for all our blessings. Thank you for blessing Nino with strength and bravery! Thank you God for giving Tony wisdom and character to hold the job he does so that I may stay home with our children. Thank you God for living in my heart because without You I would be a bitter and unhappy person. Thank you God for dying for us so one day our boys will have eternal life! For all these things, we give thanks. We hope that through our journey many of you will see the wonderful works of God. We hope that much good will come from Nino's journey. We are different people than we were before this whole thing started! Trust, believe and hope; it's that simple! Goodnight to you and yours. Our prayers are with you.

Peace and Love,

Tony and Lori

P. S. Due to the weather many were unable to make the Breakfast with Santa, and many calls were received about sending a donation! Thank you!

# Journal

The Knights of Columbus continues to accept donations. Please make checks payable to The Knights of Columbus. Their address is 1090 Franklin Street, Carlisle, PA 17013, Attn: The Nino Fund.

Next week the deposit will be made on the Therapeutic Jacuzzi. On March 28th the Knights of Columbus will hold a Boyd's Bear Bingo to try to raise the remaining funds. The total is $3,970, and we already have $1,004. WOW! Again, thank you all, and may God bless you!

12/17/03

Hi! I hope this finds you all well and happy! I really look forward to sharing good news with all of you, but sometimes I just need to vent. Tonight is one of those times. The last couple of days have been a little tough. Before we left for NIH, we were worried about where our journey was taking us; then we had the anticipation of beginning the new medicine regimen. Now, we're settled.

I am not sure many of you understand what our days are like. Let me share last night into today with you. At 3:00 AM, Nino woke up with a fever of 104.1, and was crying of a bellyache. Doesn't it make you feel good when you can help your child when they hurt? I can't! I hold him and rock him, and love him, all the while knowing I cannot make his hurt go away! He went back to sleep quickly, after taking pain medicine. He woke up this morning about 6:30 and lay on the oversized chair in the living room where he ate, watched TV, rested, and cried. He was achy and had a 106.7 fever at 7:15. I gave him a lukewarm bath, while he cried; but it brought the fever down. The nurse arrived around 8:00 to help with his ENBREL injection. (If you ever get a chance, you should visit the website and learn about this medication. It is fascinating!) So, in the chair is where we gave Nino his shot today. You can always tell when he is having a "flare". He looks very pale, tired, and weak. I will NEVER describe Nino as being WEAK. He is one of the strongest individuals I have ever had the honor to know. He has my dad's fire, my spirit, and his Daddy's strength. What a combination! Finally around noon, he asked what was for lunch! That's a great sign! He drew an Advent picture with the boys, and we read together for awhile with Angelo. Tonight he is doing fine. He's back to himself! Thanks for letting me share a day with you.

Yesterday the boys had play practice at the Shrine Church from 1:00 PM to 3:00 PM. Nino had a doctor's appointment at 2:00. Tony was on duty. I took the boys to practice, stayed for awhile, and then went over to the

*Pediatric Center. What a day!*

*There was a scene at the office. A nurse wasn't sure if she could give Nino his second flu shot since he was on Enbrel. Our doctor knew we could and should. She, of course, has researched all the information on the medication that I am injecting into my child's body twice weekly. Anyway, tempers flared. UGH! Oh, well. We are all human.*

*As I buckle Angelo into his car seat (Nino is already in his), a teenage girl passes out right in front of me on the steps exiting the Pediatric Center. I screamed for help, checked for a pulse, and comforted the poor mom who was hysterical by this point. What is that saying? "God doesn't give us more than we can handle."*

*Then, it gets better! I ran into Wal-Mart to get taco sauce because Mr. Nino requested tacos for dinner. When he asks for a special dinner, I make it! Anyway, you must remember that NINO cannot get sick. It is just dangerous if he were to catch a simple thing like a cold, so the doctor recommended that he wear a face mask. You would have thought he had four heads, six arms, twelve tails, and polka-dots! There were so many ADULTS pointing at him I wanted to scream. He hung his head each time he noticed someone looking and pointing at him. I could have been nasty; I probably should have been nasty, but I wasn't. I said a quiet prayer for those people.*

*I prayed that they will never know pain like his. I wonder if we are really*

*aware of the impact we have on each other's lives. You never know what*

*someone else is going through; you never really know someone else's story.*

*Thank you for letting me vent. Through the whole crazy day, I stopped often*

*to give thanks to God, even in line at Wal-Mart. Thanks, God, for getting*

*me through the craziness. Thanks for letting me feel Your presence, even*

*when I am on another track. Thank you for letting me share Nino's story*

*with others. Please take something from it.*

*Hear my words and step out of your "comfort zone". Grow in spirit, mind,*

*body and soul. Let me bring this to a close with a scripture verse someone*

*shared with me. "Blessed be the God and Father of our Lord Jesus Christ,*

*the Father of compassion and God of all encouragement" from 2Corinthians*

*1:3. Read this verse, even if you don't read Scripture, and figure out how*

*it applies to your own life. I trust that God is the Light of the world.*

*I continue to look to the Light for my encouragement and strength,*

*particularly on days like yesterday. He is a compassionate God who will*

*watch over Nino and take care of him. Remember, too, it is not our will, but*

# Journal

*HIS will that will be done. May God richly bless all of you. Have a good*

*evening and tell those around you how much they mean to you!*

*Fondly,*

*Lori*

Do you ever wonder sometimes what people are thinking?
Right after our first miscarriage, someone said to me, "Why
are you sad? You have three others!" I was blown away by that
comment! You must understand that all I've ever wanted to be
was a mom. This was my baby, my dream, and now it's GONE!
Sometimes people are insensitive without meaning to be.
You have to be forgiving, yet sometimes it is so difficult.
Forgiveness is necessary for your own self growth. I remember
being in the grocery store and people were staring at Nino because
he was wearing a face mask. Of course, the mother in me wanted
to knock them out! However, the Christian in me wanted to pray
for them! The fact is, unless you've been in our shoes, you just
DON'T get it! So, forgive those that make the silly comments.
How many of you have lost a loved one and heard the line, "Well,
they're in a better place"? Did you think, "SO!"? The better place
you are thinking of is here with you, not gone forever! It's tough.
It's sometimes so hurtful; all you can do is cry.

Someone very close to us said something terribly hurtful when we first began Nino's journey. It's been four years, and I still pray daily for forgiveness for the grudge that I held. I no longer hold a grudge, although I did for a long time. I realized that it just made me sad and bitter. What benefit was coming from it? You just have to let it go, and pray really hard about it! I think people are so wrapped up in themselves, they cannot see outside their circle. That is sad! So many times someone has told me about their day and how busy they are: their job is too demanding; the kids were up all night; and the one that really got to me was when a friend called me the other day angry at her mother and went on for several minutes complaining about her mom. I wanted to stop her and say, "HELLO! Do you realize how important FAMILY is?" I could go on and on about insensitive things others say. I also think how many times I have been insensitive or hurtful with or without meaning to be. All we can do is do our best, ask for forgiveness, and trust in God.

# Journal

12/25/03

Merry Christmas to all!

We hope your Christmas was beautiful, full of family and friends. Our day was perfect! We are together and very blessed and thankful!

The boys had a wonderful morning with their surprises. The older ones still believe in Santa, and Nino was so anxious for his arrival. Angelo was so funny ripping the wrapping paper! I do think we were very aware of the real reason for the season this year. Jesus is alive in our hearts! His presence has been amazing to us these last few months. Again I remembered what Our Holy Mother endured, and this thought strengthened my belief that we can handle Nino's crisis.

The Enbrel has really seemed to help with his joint pain; actually it has been a miracle. The last episode he had of joint pain was last week, and that was just minor stiffness.

I want to thank all of you for making Christmas a little more special for us this year.

On Tuesday we drove to York and ordered the Jacuzzi for Nino! It will be delivered in 3-4 weeks. Your generosity has made such a difference in Nino's health. I am sure, unless you have been in our sort of situation, you cannot *understand our gratitude! We have been battling the insurance company for almost three years about paying for the Jacuzzi. In a few days, everything changed. I want you to know how good people are. You should look for the good in others! Pray for each other, reach out to each other. No matter what you may think, you really never know someone else's story!*

*Joe served midnight Mass on Christmas Morning! We were so PROUD! You should have seen him. I beamed the entire Mass, and Tony just watched every move he made. He felt so honored to be asked to serve at this Mass, and we were honored to be his parents. The best part about this is the pride that he felt. He talked about it all day. The other boys were talking about Santa, and Joe talked about Mass and how "cool" it was that he was selected to serve. Father Waltersheid mentioned his family Christmas Eve tradition was to go outside and locate the first star of the night. He said, "Keep your eyes fixed on that star! That star, my friends, is Jesus! Look to HIM, trust in HIM, believe in HIM!" We believe that Jesus has been our strength on our journey.*

*Let us bring this to a close by thanking all of you for so many things, mostly though, for sharing this experience with us. Thank you for telling us you have found inspiration from our story. Thank you for stepping out of your* comfort zone and going above and beyond. Thank you for being kind, loving

people who are so dear to us.

Goodnight! Merry Christmas!

Peace and Love to you and yours,

Tony and Lori

Marc and Aunt Honey ~ Thank you!

Father Waltersheid ~ Thank you!

Robin, Earl, and kids ~ Christmas was beautiful! Our "discussion" was so

cool!


12/31/03

HAPPY NEW YEAR!

Good evening, everyone!

Can you believe 2004 is just around the corner? It has been an amazing year

for many of us. I just wanted to take a few minutes and send a message to

all of you.

Today was a crazy day! My mom was admitted to Carlisle Hospital. Her

lungs are not strong, and she is having a lot of difficulty with her breathing.

She has been ill for quite some time, and we are thankful for all the "extra" time God has lent her to us. Please keep her in your prayers. Also, a dear

friend of mine gave birth this morning. Monica Ann was born around 5:00

this morning, and she and her mommy are doing terrific! Please keep them in

your prayers, too!

I am going to get the snacks and "bubbly" ready for Tony and the boys and

me to share at midnight. Believe it or not, this is the first New Year's Eve

that we can remember that Tony is not on duty! I usually wake the boys

around 11:45, and we bring in the New Year with a toast using ginger

ale, of course! They even get to use the nice wine glasses! If Tony is on a

midnight shift, he calls; if he is on second shift (3:00 PM to 11.00 PM), he

usually gets home just in time.

Before I get the goodies ready, I wanted to share some thoughts with you. The

Enbrel is working wonders for Nino's joint pain! Whatever stiffness he still

has, the Jacuzzi will take care of; the Jacuzzi will be here in the next couple

of weeks. Even though he has been running a fever for two days, 100-104, he

actually has been coping so well. Today was a shot day; he just rolled up his

pants and said "It's right leg, today!" We have to alternate injection sites so

he has quickly learned his left from his right. What a way to teach it, huh?

# Journal

I cannot tell you what your kindness and generosity has meant to our family! We have been so blessed and feel so grateful! We have grown so much through this last year. I pray that all of you have experienced joy this year. I pray that you experience real love and peace this New Year. My hope is that many of you will open your hearts to the Lord. Let HIM come into your lives and trust in HIM. I don't know where our journey is going; I know that God is with us, we have each other, and we are on our way!

Be good to each other. Love, trust, and hope.

HAPPY NEW YEAR!

We love you all.

Fondly,

Tony, Lori, and boys

Holly ~ Thanks for returning the crock pot.

Aunt Honey and Marc ~ You have made such a difference!

Mr. and Mrs. O ~ Thanks!


1/04/04

Hi there!

Here's to hoping your New Year has been amazing so far. Today we received an incredible email from a special friend. She asked what church we attend.

She went on to say that our story has inspired her to begin attending church,

or as she put it, "get my butt in gear"! We believe that you all have inspired

us much more than you realize.

Well, the last few days have been tough for Nino. He developed an upper

respiratory infection and has had a difficult time. Due to his immune system

being suppressed, we have to be more careful. When he gets a virus, his

arthritis becomes severe. Also, his fevers spike quickly and last several days.

Friday around 3:00 he got really sick. He had a fever of 106; he wasn't able

to get around, and he was crying, "OUCH!". The times when we want to

make the hurt go away, and we can't, are so difficult for us! We took turns

holding him and comforting him. By midnight he finally fell asleep. Tony

and Angelo were asleep in our bed, and I stayed with Nino. He woke up

again around 1:30 AM with a 106.9 fever and uncontrollable tears. Off to

the hospital we went. I think every Emergency Room doctor knows Nino!

Of course, they just love him! The nurse who took his blood must have been

new, as she wondered if an additional person was needed to "hold" Nino

while she drew the blood. Are you kidding? Nino is a pro at this. Nino even

informed her from what arm he preferred her to draw the blood. The nurse just looked at me like as if to say, "Is he for real?" Of course, I'm thinking, just take the blood already! Anyway, we arrived home around 5:30 AM, and we were beat! Nino fell asleep around 7:00 AM, and the day began with the others. Tony took Vinny to his basketball game at 8:00. His team lost, but Vinny played well! Nino was upset that he missed his game scheduled for 10:00. I got to take Joey to his game at 2:00; Saint Pat's lost by four points, but you should have seen Joe play. He was awesome! Anyway, Nino has taken it easy the last couple of days, and I'm sure he'll go right to sleep tonight. I hope in the morning he is bouncing around again!

On Wednesday, January 7th, we will be going to Lancaster to consult with a Pediatric Gastroenterologist. He will decide if there is something that can be done for the stomach ulcers and problems Nino has with his belly. There are days that he goes without eating and does not drink much either! Hopefully the doctor will know what to do.

Our next visit to NIH is the first week of February. I believe it is February 2nd-5th. Joey's birthday is February 3rd, and this will be the first time I will not be with him when he wakes up on his birthday.

Birthday mornings are big deals in our house. I hang streamers or toot horns or something and always have some small gift waiting for them. They also say they hate that I wake them up singing "Happy Birthday"! If you have ever heard me sing, you understand! God has blessed me with wonderful gifts; unfortunately a good singing voice is not one of them!

Tony is now officially a Knight with the Knights of Columbus. I am so proud of him! He attended a special ceremony today and was very excited! The Knights is a Catholic men's group. They do wonderful works for the community!

Well, I should bring this to a close. A friend of ours has been in the hospital. She is home now, but is still having a lot of problems. She is the mother of three little boys and is a beautiful person. Please keep that family in your prayers.

Please continue to pray for Nino. I am amazed by his character. I am telling you, God has something incredible planned for him! You know, the other day when I was working on NO sleep, I felt so run down. I started to complain to Tony that I needed some rest. I caught myself and thought, Nino does this regularly, even times that I don't realize. I will often wake up in the middle of the night and find Nino watching TV because his legs hurt, and he can't sleep. So, c'mon! Who am I to complain about being a little tired?

God Bless you all. Be good to each other. Open your hearts.

*Love and Peace,*

*Tony and Lori*

*Holly ~ THANKS!*


*1/07/04*

*Hi, everyone!*

*I just wanted to give you the news about the appointment we had today.*

*ANOTHER surgical procedure is needed, unfortunately! We were very*

*happy with the doctor; he seemed very knowledgeable about Nino's*

*condition. Another thing that really impressed us was that he talked to*

*Nino. He directed all of his words to the three of us. That matters. You may*

*think that Nino is only five, but he knows his body; and he understands a*

*lot more than you may think! Do you know when he uses a public bathroom*

*he carries his wipes with him? Do you know that he won't share cups,*

*straws, dishes, or food with anyone, not even his brothers! His famous*

*question now is, "Does this have germs?" Believe me; he deserves to be*

*spoken to by doctors, and everyone else for that matter. IT IS HIS BODY!*

*Anyway, enough of that!*

# Journal

*Dr. Devenyi in Lancaster believes doing an endoscopy is the best thing right now! They will biopsy some of the ulcers, and anything else that they find! Also, depending on the results they receive from Hershey this week, they may do a colonoscopy at the same time. This will be his fourth surgical procedure for which he has been sedated! That is the scary part for us. Usually, we are allowed to bring him into the operating room until the sedation takes effect, and he falls asleep. It is NOT a good feeling to leave your child on a table, alone, looking helpless. Please know we are in GREAT hands, and we trust all of his physicians; but he is still our baby!*

*Here is the list of upcoming dates, so you can keep Nino in your prayers. Friday, January 16th, we are in Hershey for a follow-up appointment. Wednesday through Friday, February 4 - 6, we are at NIH for our return visit. Tuesday, February 10th at 7:15 AM we will arrive at the Surgery Center in Lancaster, PA, because Nino's surgery is scheduled for 8:15 AM. Tuesday, February 17th, we have our follow-up appointment in Lancaster. This is when we will learn the biopsy results, and Nino will have whatever other testing he may need! So, that is what's coming up! Please keep him in your prayers. Our wonderful friend Andrea has made arrangements for meals, and the boys' coaches have arranged for rides to and from basketball*

*practices. Thank you everyone.*

*My mom is not in the best of health, but she takes care of the other boys*

*while we are with Nino. It means a great deal that she IS able to help!*

*However, it takes a toll on her; so the meals are a HUGE help! Again, thank*

*you. If you are in the area and want to stop by to see if she needs anything,*

*that is also a big help!*

*Again, let me remind you that our faith is getting us through. You know,*

*someone said to me the other day, "I don't know how you do it! I couldn't*

*be that strong!" Believe me, we have our moments; but we just have to trust*

*in the LORD! No matter what happens, there is more to this story. There*

*IS the bigger picture. Much good has come from this. Nino is an amazing*

*person, our faith IS stronger than ever, and our boys are compassionate and*

*kind. Tony and I lean on each other now more than ever!*

*You have all been so generous and kind. If you take things for granted*

*in your life and think you are above it all, you have lost sight of the real*

*importance of the time you have. I see a fire in Nino, a thrill in life. He is*

*always seeking challenges, and overcoming them! He always does his best, even when it hurts! That is how I want to live. I need to be the best I can be*

*so that one day I will stand before the Lord and say I did my very best!*

*I hope this finds you well and hope your New Year has been wonderful so*

*far. Thank you for caring so much!*

*God bless.*

*Fondly,*

*Tony and Lori*

As I travel on the journey through the rough yet sometimes still waters I never lose sight of the shore. My boys are always present with their watchful eyes. They are the destination; I want to reach them with truth, morals, passion and love!

WOW!

What an incredible honor to be the mom of four sons. It is
wonderful to see the boys interact with each other. I longed for
that as a child. They grow so quickly, too quickly. I cherish each
of them differently. They are so different from each other, yet so
similar. I am so impressed by their courage. They lift me up so
high. As I watch them help with Nino on a bad day, I am blessed
by their compassion. When I watch them playfully tackle him on
good days, I am comforted by their normalcy.

On our journeys to the Children's Inn, I watch their reactions to the
different children they meet. You know what I see? I see nothing
out of the ordinary. They meet, greet, and make friends with
everyone and anyone.

I hope this life experience is teaching them compassion for Nino,
as well as for others. I hope Tony and I are teaching them about
the importance of love and commitment. As I watch them travel on
this journey, I am proud of the sensitive, compassionate, flexible,
and understanding men they are becoming. I don't think they will

ever know the depths of my love for them, or the privilege I feel to

be their mother!

Thank you, God, for their beautiful gift in my life.

# Journal

1/29/04

Good morning!

We have SO much to tell you. Things have been busy around here, as I am sure it is for all of you. How are you enjoying the snow? It is beautiful, BUT how many more days 'til SPRING?

Nino was so excited yesterday when the delivery truck with his Jacuzzi pulled in the driveway! Our friend Mac will do the wiring as soon as we can get back to him with a time that is good for us. The Jacuzzi, which is a huge blessing, will then be up and running!

On Monday, Nino built snow forts with the boys and their friends. He was running a fever on Tuesday and Wednesday, so he just watched. His appetite has not been the greatest, but it did not stop him from wanting to play in the snow. It's sad but true. We want him to be as normal as possible, but the situation is not a normal one!

The March for Life was amazing. It was cold, and the march itself was quite a distance; but the life experience was unbelievable! During part of the march we prayed the rosary, hundreds of us. The boys talked about that! Joe thought it was so cool that so many people came from all over the country "to save babies"! I thought it was "cool" to see the boys' reaction. Vinny's *favorite part was hearing President George Bush speak! The President was in New Mexico but called in to the rally, and Vinny thought that was great!*

*Mitzi took care of Nino and Angelo and said everything went well. The boys just love spending time with her! Thanks, Mitzi!*

*Unfortunately, my mom is not well. She is actually not doing any better. We have decided to take the boys with us to NIH. Many friends have offered to help, and Tony's brother and his wife have offered to drive to Carlisle and get the boys and take them back to Mt. Union for the week. We so appreciate the offers from all of you but have decided to take them with us. It is hard to be at NIH trying to focus on what we need to do and worry about the boys back home. Tony and I will "tag team" back and forth to the hospital, but we will all stay together at the Children's Inn. Thursday morning one of us will take Nino over to the hospital for the morning tests. In between testing, we will return to the Inn and trade off. The same will happen Friday. Please pray that all goes well. They may want to change the dose of Nino's current medication or add another one. Things have been going better with his joint pain, but he is still having a lot of fevers and a lot of stomach problems. As for the surgery date, we have NOT figured that out YET!*

# Journal

Mitzi again has offered to keep the other boys, but we are not sure how we will get the boys to her house. We have to leave Carlisle around 5:15 AM because Lancaster is about one hour from our home. With the winter weather, we need to allow more time. The surgery is scheduled for 6:45 AM, so we were hoping to let the boys sleep in and have someone here to help them get ready when they wake up and take them to Mitzi's! Please continue to pray that all of this works out.

The Boyd's Bear Bingo is planned for March 28th at 2:00 PM and will be held at The Knights of Columbus Hall in Carlisle! Tickets are being printed, and ticket orders are currently being taken. Tickets are $20 each. Please let us know how many tickets you'd like! We have flyers if you'd like to pass some out! We have already taken some orders; there are about one hundred twenty seats available, so reserve your place early!

Well, we should bring this note to a close for now. We want to thank all of you for your continual support! You all have made such a difference in our lives. You know, God never leaves you. God always protects you, and God always loves you! Sometimes we may not see the hand of God in every situation, but we promise you that if you look for it, it's there!

# Journal

We continue to pray for all of you. We also continue to pray for our growth through this difficult time. May the Lord bless us and keep us, and may He always bless you and your families!

Make it a great day!

Fondly,

Tony and Lori


2/01/04

Good evening, friends!

I am not sure where to begin tonight, but I really felt the need to share with you.

It is Sunday evening, and the boys are asleep. Tony is glued to the Super Bowl; and the house is quiet, except for some outbursts from Tony, of course! We will be taking the boys to NIH with us. That is going to be an adventure. We will work hard toward making this trip another positive life experience for us as a family. WOW, the things we all have experienced this year.

We have been thinking about sending the boys back to Saint Patrick School next year! It was a wonderful learning environment for so many years for them and for us. We really grew as a family through our experiences there!

I am torn, though; because home schooling has also been very rewarding!

Academically, it has been incredible, but we faced a battle with our school

district regarding service availability for Nino. Because we home school the

boys, our district will NOT provide speech and physical therapy for Nino.

At Saint Patrick School he will receive these special services, which will be a

huge blessing! Also, I think the boys will benefit from being out and feeling

"normal" again.

This school year has been quite confusing for all of us. It is great that we

have had such special time together, especially on the rough days! We hope

the boys have really learned the value of family! We will continue to pray

about our decision.

The next few weeks are going to be difficult! I am a little frightened, to be

very honest! I do not like the idea of anesthesia, again! I don't like seeing

Nino suffer after the procedures. I don't like holding him when he has the

terrible reaction while he is coming out of the sedation, but hopefully this

procedure will bring some answers. We will travel to Lancaster on the 17th

to hear about the biopsy results. I will absolutely keep you posted.

# Journal

*I am a little concerned about our visit to NIH. Nino's joint pain is doing a little better, but his fevers still occur on a regular basis. He has had no seizures since December, though! Also, his belly problems have gotten worse. He has a lot of difficulty eating! His appetite comes and goes. The weird thing is that when he is hungry, he knows exactly what he wants; and he eats ALL of it!*

*By the way, he played in his basketball game on Saturday and made a basket! YEAH!*

*I must tell you about a parenting call we made. Nino has been running a fever all week. He has also really been complaining about back pain due to the arthritis in his lower back, knees, and feet. He has been talking about his game ALL week; so on Saturday morning, after he got his injection, we gave him pain medicine (Tylenol with codeine) just so he could play in his game! If some of you think that is insane, let me ask you, "How often has your child asked you to make their legs or back stop hurting?" I cannot tell you how many times Nino misses something or we have had to change plans for him, due to pain. Our pediatrician, and friend, put it very simply to me awhile ago. She said, "Will he remember that he had to have pain medicine to get through a soccer game, or will he remember how good it felt to play?"*

# Journal

That, my friends, is the reality! One day, I pray that Nino will look back on his childhood (as he is holding one of his own children in his arms, or is in the Seminary, Ha-Ha!) and know that we did the very best we could and that we loved him with every breath we took!

This is a very difficult situation in which to be. Our faith is incredibly strong, our friends are just amazing, our commitment to each other and our boys is powerful, but it is still TOUGH! The last few days I have been pretty down. I am not sure why. I think it is the anticipation about what is to come. I said the other day to a friend, "I feel as though the world continues to spin around us and we are suspended somewhere!" I don't really know what I mean by that. I know it is a feeling. I want so much to change things and go back to our lives as they were before, BUT we are such different people now! We are REAL people now. We understand what really matters. We "get it"!

I wish you could really watch Nino sometimes. It is an amazing sight. He just does what he has to do. The other evening he was really hurting. His fever was 105.0. He "hobbled" down the stairs and climbed on the sofa with Tony. He took Tony's hand and put it on his back. I watched this whole scene. Then Tony looked him in the eyes and started to rub his back. It truly was a father-son moment. It may not be a moment that you may have with

your sons; but, for them, just a small glance said everything.

Well, I should bring this to a close. I have been trying my best to keep our

updates short and informative. Tonight, I really wanted to express some

thoughts. You continue to be in our prayers. I have tried to send thank you

notes to many of you. Thank you for the meals, the donations to The Knights

of Columbus, the calls, the cards, etc. If I have failed to get a note to you,

please accept my apologies.

We are SO very thankful to each and every one of you! Your prayers

continue to make a difference. Your kind words and deeds really touch our

hearts. May you feel the presence of God in your lives and in your hearts as

well.

Love,

Lori


2/11/04

Hi, everyone!

Yesterday was an okay day. It was not as difficult as I expected. I don't

know if it's because we are getting "used" to all of these appointments and procedures or what! I hope not, but maybe it is not a bad thing. I guess

we can call it acceptance. Please God help me to accept the things I cannot

change.

Robin went with Nino and me. It was great to have her there. She is

one of my best friends. It was so cool how she found a way to debate my

Republican views and harass me about George Bush, all the while making

me laugh while we waited for Nino to come out of the operating room.

That's what good friends do: challenge you; support you; be there for you;

and love you unconditionally, even if they are Democrats (got you Robin!)!

Well, the procedure went well. Nino is so brave; sometimes I just am amazed

by his strength!

The doctor found a lot of scar tissue in his belly, which is not unexpected

due to the ulcers from the medicines he has been taking. Around the ulcers,

though, there is some inflammation. They took some of that tissue to biopsy,

just to be sure. Also, they found a "mass" of enlarged lymph nodes in his

colon, so they also took some tissue samples of that to biopsy.

Mrs. O took care of the boys at home, and they had a blast! You should see

their art work for their book report. It was awesome! (Thanks, Mrs. O.) Joey

wrote a poem titled "THE LITTLE HERO" which was chosen for the local *newspaper. It will touch your heart! It is about his little brother Nino, and*

*how proud he is of him. If you do not get the paper and you'd like a copy,*

*please let us know!*

*Tonight there is a prayer service at the Shrine Church. It is the feast day of*

*Our Lady of Lourdes. If you remember, that is who we have been offering*

*prayers to for Nino's healing.*

*Tony and I will return to Lancaster on the 17th to learn the results. I think,*

*the waiting for that day is harder than the waiting for the procedure day.*

*We will not take any of the boys with us. If we receive good news, we will*

*celebrate! If the news is not good, we will have each other and the time to*

*take in all the information we are given! So, that is the plan. Keep in mind*

*our return visit to NIH the first week of March!*

*We are doing okay. Our prayers are focused on next Tuesday. I feel very*

*uneasy about the mass that the doctor found. I pray that whatever we hear*

*next week, we are able to find something to help Nino. I pray that we never*

*lose sight of the big picture, that we never take anything for granted, and*

*that I always remember the very first visit to NIH and how humbled we*

*were. I continue to pray for strength and God's grace on me as a MOM.*

# Journal

Andrea brought over a casserole that the boys loved. Mitzi brought over a pot of soup that was to die for! You guys are such a blessing in our lives. I cannot thank you enough! Thank you for all of the meals that have been made for us the last few days! When you drop off a meal, please leave a note with your name and address so that I can send thank you cards. It makes it easier to keep things straight. Oh, Shelia, Tony raved about your casserole. Anita, the ziti was terrific. Lisa, Vinny loved your lasagna! Did I forget anyone?

Well, I should bring this to a close for now. I wanted to let you know how the procedure went last night, but we were just too tired!

This Sunday at Mass, we sang my very favorite song, "BE NOT AFRAID". When I sing it or hear it, I feel as though God is speaking right to me: "Be not afraid, I go before you always. Come follow me, and I will give you rest!" Believe me; HE is right next to us. The strength you see in us is not about how strong we are, but about our faith in God.

Whatever direction our life's journey takes us, we are not afraid for HE goes before us always. We continue to follow HIM and love our family and others on our way.

Thanks to all of you.

# Journal

*Take care of yourselves and each other.*

*Lori*

*Mr. Kilmore ~ The cake was perfect!*

*Marc ~ Enjoy every second.*

*Holly ~ Thanks!*

*P. S. Our piano teacher has donated the Boyd's Bear Bingo tickets at no cost to the fundraiser. Tickets are now available. We have already sold many! There are only one hundred ten available, and I think we have already sold almost forty.*

*Mark your calendar for March 28th at 2.00 PM. THANKS!*

# A Little Hero

My brother is a little hero,
he is really strong and brave.
When Mom gives him his shot,
he never, ever complains.
He has good days and bad,
on good days we play alot.
On his bad days,
which are sad, he cannot.
I'm the oldest of four brothers,
I like to take care of them.
I'm really proud of Nino,
and will look up to him til the end!

By: Joey Todaro - Age 10 ~ Homeschool
29 West I st. Carlisle, PA. 17013     Kids World due Jan. 28th (Poems)

# Journal

02/16/04

*Hello!*

*It's late in the evening, or really early in the morning, whichever you prefer. It has been a tough couple of days for us. Not only has Nino been having a tough time, but Angelo is teething and feeling pretty yucky! The lack of sleep is causing Mom to be less patient and downright tough with Joe and Vinny. Today we made a real effort to have some quiet time for just the three of us (Joe, Vinny and me). We started reading Lord of the Flies. It is truly one of the best books I have ever read; although it is definitely above the boys' reading level, I love to share great literature with them and take time to share thoughts along the way!*

*We also went to Mass tonight, just the three of us. Today marks the beginning of the most amazing season for Christians, LENT! Also, today is the big day of the official release of The Passion of the Christ. How many of you saw it? What did you think? I heard many in the media say it was too gory! One reporter today said, "There was too much violence!" I haven't seen the movie YET, but how can the crucifixion of a man NOT be violent? As I sat in Mass tonight with the boys, I thought about the incredible honor* given to all of us as parents; we mold these little people into the men and women they become. Isn't that an amazing responsibility?

Awhile back, Tony and I had to make a tough decision regarding Nino and his playing in a soccer game. It was a terrible morning for him. He asked for pain medicine so that he could play in his game without his legs hurting. Well, we did give him the medicine; and he played his little heart out! He still talks about how many goals he scored that day.

Each day all of us make decisions for our children; each day we are examples for them. Each day they grow before our eyes. I asked someone just recently, "Where does the time go?" Friends, it goes too quickly!

We have learned so many valuable life lessons on our journey, but the one that matters most to us is to never waste a single moment! God has given each of us a very precious gift of life. Whether you are seventy-five, fifty, or five, when your time here on earth is over, it's over; so you must make the most of each day! That is a lesson we learn from Jesus himself! He didn't care what others said about Him. He didn't worry about what would happen. He had a purpose, just as each of us does. We must step out of our comfort zones! We must be the very best that God intended us to be, every moment! Enjoy the gift of life, even on bad days!

# *Journal*

*I should bring this to a close for tonight. I wanted to share some thoughts with you. Thanks for letting me vent. Thanks again for sharing this journey with us. If one person has taken an extra moment to tell someone how very much they mean, or if one of you has gone to church for the first time in a long time, or if one of you has offered up a prayer, we feel our story has made a difference. We are blessed to have you in our lives. We are blessed with our boys. If it were not for Nino's journey, Tony and I would still be searching without meaning. God bless you all!*

*Peace and Love,*

*Tony and Lori*


*2/17/04*

*Good morning!*

*It's about 6:30. The house is quiet, and the boys are still asleep. They usually get up at 7:30 to get ready for their school day! Tony has already left for work; he will meet me at the appointment today. The dogs are asleep at my feet. I don't know whether to cry, sigh, laugh or scream!*

*The last two days have been tough. Nino has had a flare, with a lot of pain in his back and legs, a fever, and belly pain, as well as the infamous rash! He* was up and down a lot during the night, but the pain medicine helped! It is hard to watch when he is in so much pain and to know that I cannot take it away.

The easy part of this whole thing is watching when Nino feels well. He is so happy and energetic! He seems like a normal, typical, healthy, five-year-old boy! He is tackling his brothers and playing sports! Have you ever seen Nino play a soccer or basketball game? When he's feeling up to it, look out!

I just wanted to send a message out to keep you posted. Many friends called or emailed yesterday; so many just said they loved us and were praying for us. They really didn't know what else to say. One friend called and just said, "I have no idea what to say, but I had to call." Thanks! Sometimes we don't know what to say to you. This is all part of our life. This is the way it is! We are real people, and great things happen in our lives every day! Don't feel like you always have to ask about Nino; we have three other sons about whom you can ask. Ask about Tony's job, gymnastics, etc… Thanks for being wonderful friends who have made such a difference in our lives.

We don't know what we will learn at the appointment today. Am I nervous? Absolutely! I have been on the verge of tears since last Tuesday. Although, I know my tears will not change anything! We can't change anything. There is an ultimate plan. We may not understand the whys or the hows; we just have to live on FAITH alone. Our faith is what is getting us through!

I am going to end for now. I am going to have a cup of tea and get my lesson plans ready, as my poor mother is going to play teacher again today. God bless her! I hope you all have a blessed day! We will get news to you as soon as we can. All you do is SO appreciated, but the fact that so many of you care has made all the difference to us!

Love,

Lori

Heather ~ We are praying for you, too! Thanks for everything!

Tracy ~ Thanks for "getting it" yesterday. You make me laugh. ☺

Andrea ~ Thanks for the milk, and everything else!

Dave and Nina ~ Thanks for taking the boys to Physics; they loved it!


2/17/04

Hi! I just wanted to send a quick note to share the good news.

There are no malignancies! It is indeed believed that Nino's symptoms are caused by a genetic disorder, and Dr. Devenyi has pointed us in another direction. Nino has inflammation throughout his body. That is why he has a fever, rash, joint pain, and the inflammation in the lining of his intestines.

That may not sound good, but it is a clue to what's happening!

We are at Hershey tomorrow, and Nino has an ultrasound of his belly on Friday morning at 7:00 AM. Next week we are doing some fun stuff and hanging out as a family! The following week we are off again to NIH.

As we learn more, we will keep you posted. See, I told you to trust God. We do! Be good to each other. Count your blessings, and tonight, count them twice.

Thanks for being on this journey with us.

Fondly,

Tony and Lori

# Letter from a Friend

Hi everyone!

Some of you know me; others do not. I'm a friend of the Todaro family, and I read Lori's updates regularly. Sometimes I dread opening the updates because of how helpless I feel when I read about all this family is going through.

It's easy to forget about their troubles when you run into them at the grocery store, sporting events, church, etc.; and they look so happy and healthy.

But as you know them from the emails, their family life at home is not as easy as most of ours. They meet new challenges every day, and some days Lori and Tony have to deal with these challenges with very little rest. I'm sure there are days when they wonder how they will go on another day, even if they don't say this!

These are the days when the Todaros could use the help of their friends!

I'm sure, like me, many of you wonder what you can do to help; but you don't know where to begin.

# Letter from a Friend

It's easy. Here are some ideas I got from Lori:

- If you enjoy cooking, make a meal and take it to them. Lori's not having to worry about preparing dinner would be a huge relief; and it could mean she can spend more time caring for or playing with the kids.

- If you're healthy (because we don't want to infect their household), stop by and offer to spend some time entertaining the kids, helping around the house or just visiting.

- If you've got kids to chauffeur to and from the YMCA, sports events, etc., call and offer to take the boys along.

- If you're headed to Giant or Wal-Mart, call Lori and ask if she needs anything.

- Offer to baby-sit for an hour or two some night so Lori and Tony can get out.

# Letter from a Friend

- Pick up the phone and call Lori, Tony and the boys. Let them know you care. Ask them if there's anything you can do.

- Send the boys cards just to encourage them and to tell them you're thinking about them.

- Pray for them. If we all take a few minutes out of our busy lives to nurture the Todaros, they'll be grateful; and we'll be helping out friends who need us.

Thanks for reading,

Andrea

It is sometimes so tiring trying to reach the shore. Many times along the way, I grab on to the vine to pull myself along. Friends are always there, lending a hand, lending support, lending their love.

I have learned a lot about friendship on this journey.

First, many people will enter and exit your life. Many will be acquaintances; few will be friends. So many wonderful people are a part of our lives today, or have been in the past. Each day is a new beginning. Those you share today with may not be here tomorrow. You cannot control anyone else but yourself, which is important to remember. Some very special people in my life are no longer friends. Times change. People change. We all move forward.

It is sad sometimes to loose friends, especially those that are close to you. You again have no control over that. Just be who you are, and be the best that you can be.

Some people have a tough time accepting tragedy. Some people cannot talk with me about Nino; it's easier for them not to hear about it at all. I think it is too close to home. No Mom ever wants to think about something being wrong with her child. The fact is that some people are only friends until times get tough. That's when you learn who is really a true friend.

We have been so blessed with so many kind and wonderful people

in our lives, but we can probably count on our hands the true

friends we have. It is just the way life is. Every individual

that you meet along the way shapes the person you are becoming.

Always be grateful for others in your life. Try to be a good friend,

try to be a good listener, and above all else stay true to yourself.

# Letters from Friends

2/27/04

Hello to all!

My name is Stephanie, and I am Lori's sister-in-law. I just got a call from Lori, and she had some horrible news. Her mother, Lorraine, passed away this morning. It was definitely unexpected! Lori is DEVASTATED! Most of you know that Lori is an only child, and her father passed away several years ago; so her mother was all she had left. I am going to do all that I can; but with my not living very close, it's hard. I am asking all of you to keep Lori, Anthony, and the boys in your prayers! I don't know what else to say. I am still in shock! I will email as soon as I know any details. If any of you would like to get in touch with me....

Sincerely,

Stephanie

# Letters from Friends

2/27/04

Hi,

I am a friend of Lori's and also knew her mother. How

horrible for her!

Please let us know more details as they come along

Thank you,

Barb


2/27/04

Hi Stephanie,

I know Lori through my daughter. She taught my daughter

gymnastics, and we have stayed in touch through emails

and have seen each other around town, as I also live

in Carlisle. Thanks for letting all of us know about Lori's

mother. I can't imagine what Lori is going through. I will

keep her and her family in my prayers.

Thanks again!

Laurie

# Letters from Friends

2/27/04

Thank you, Stephanie.

I'd like to suggest that those of us who live near the Todaros, and are able to do so, take dinner to them. I will volunteer for Monday (that's March 1st). If anyone else reading this would like to volunteer for a specific day, please send a message using the "reply all" button, and just add your day on to the list. I'd suggest we aim for dinner delivered every other day for two weeks. Try to make rather large dinners, so they will have leftovers. That has been one of the nicest things people have done for my family when we have had a death to endure. We were just in too much of a fog of grief to cook. With four hungry boys, well, that would be a good opportunity to help.

Angie

# Letters from Friends

2/27/04

Wait a second, everybody.

Angie, that's a great idea, but I think meals were already

planned for some of those days because they were

supposed to be at NIH with Nino. I think that Andrea

may have already organized meals for those days.

Perhaps you can touch base with her SO that there isn't

duplication.

Kathy


2/27/04

At this point, Lori and Tony are going to NIH as scheduled

next week, on Tuesday, which is a change from what they

thought they were doing earlier today, after discovering

it would be April before they could reschedule. They are

taking the four boys with them.

Holly

# Letters from Friends

Hello everyone,

First of all I wanted to say thank you for all of the reply emails that I have received from people wanting to help and offering their prayers. Your prayers mean so much to Anthony, Lori, and the boys! I have forwarded all of them to Tony and Lori, and they have read them and appreciate all of your support. They are also thankful for all of the meals and flowers that were brought, and for the cards sent from everyone. I was down on Saturday for the day to help out with the boys so that Tony and Lori could get some things finalized. Lori is holding up well, but I think that she is still in shock. They have so much to do and to finalize, and then with Nino's visit to NIH coming up in the next few days, she really hasn't had time to digest everything. PLEASE keep her and her family in your prayers!

This week is going to be especially hard for her with trying to cope with her loss and with thinking about going

# Letters from Friends

to NIH, so say another prayer that everything goes well

for Nino!

I know that a lot of you were asking about funeral plans,

wanted to know when things would be, and what you

could do to help out. I do have some information to pass

along to all of you. Father Waltersheid is going to do

a Memorial Mass on Friday, March 5th at 10:30 AM at

the Shrine Church, 140 East Pomfret Street, Carlisle.

Immediately following the Mass, there will be a luncheon

at the Knights of Columbus Hall, 1090 Franklin Street,

Carlisle.

Lori was an only child, and her father passed away

several years ago; so she has no family to be there to

help support her. Craig and I will be there, and hopefully

some others from Tony's family will be able to attend. If

any of you are able to make it to the Mass, that would

GREAT! After their week at NIH in combination with

the loss of Lori's mother, they will definitely need your

support, now more than ever.

# Letters from Friends

Some of you also asked about sending flowers, etc. All

contributions can be made to The Knights of Columbus

Council 4057.

If anyone has any other questions, you can email me.

Again I want to thank you for the prayers and your

willingness to help. Tony and Lori also thank you.

Sincerely,

Stephanie

# Journal

3/04/04

Dear Friends,

We are at NIH with Nino.

My heart hurts! I feel tired and drained, and empty. My mom died on Friday, February 27, 2004. It is believed that she died in her sleep and peacefully. I swore after my dad's death that I would be with my mom when she died, but I was not. I am not sure she would have let go so willingly if I had been there! How am I? I am not really sure. There is so much to do right now. I am very busy and have not had any down time to really think about things. Each time we have returned from the hospital, I have thought to call her. I cannot tell you how sad I am. I cannot think of a day without her, as you know there have already been several. Many of you have lost parents and have shared your story with me. Thank you. I don't know what to say to any of you. Tony and I are so blessed to have so many wonderful friends. There are so many return calls to make. What do I say?

You know, when I share the updates, I just type how I feel, which is what I am doing now. If I am babbling, I apologize. I hurt all over, yet I feel I must be strong for my boys, as they have lost a huge part of their life. For those of you who knew my mom, she was one like no other! I have been so blessed to have shared thirty-four years with her. My children are better people because of the gift she was in their lives. My husband is a better man because of her constant love and support!

I thank all of you for your kindness; it means much more than I could ever express.

Our visit at NIH is going well. Nino was fitted for orthopedic insoles, which are going to be great support for his legs and feet. The speech evaluator was terrific! She has pointed us in the right direction and has suggested that we contact the Intermediate Unit about getting weekly speech therapy for Nino at home. The neurologist doesn't see a need for an MRI; he thinks Nino is on target and will only need some follow-up with the Occupational Therapist, Physical Therapist, and Speech Therapist/Clinician, which we already anticipated. The Genetic Counselor was also wonderful.

They are doing a chromosomal test tomorrow. The results will hopefully provide direction for us. We will consult with Dr. Kastner in the morning about Nino's new medicine regimen, which is a concern for us, as we want him to be as comfortable and as functional as possible!

I hope that this note filled you in about our visit. We miss our boys TERRIBLY! Angelo misses his dad. He is a true Daddy's boy, and Tony wouldn't have it any other way. I am sure Joe and Vinny have a heavy heart. I wish I were with them right now, just for a hug.

# Journal

*I am not very sure what God has planned for me. I wonder sometimes why HE trusts me so much. I think I cannot take one more thing, and yet there it is! I don't know why! Who am I to question?*

*My mom isn't hurting any longer. She is probably in my dad's arms right now. Can you imagine that reunion?*

*I will miss her every moment for the rest of my life, but I will go on. I will hurt, and I will go on. I will be the very best Mom I can be, the very best wife I can be, and the very best woman I can be, for my mom's sake. I hope she and my dad are proud.*

*Each update I tell all of you not to take one second for granted. I remind you of that tonight. Please tell those around you how very much they mean to you. We are not here forever. Go above and beyond. Love God, love yourself, and love others. It's all we have friends.*

*As I bring this to a close, please know how much your love and support means to me.*

*May God bless you and keep you.*

*Fondly,*

*Lori*

The journey was always safe with my mom's arms around me.

I wore her strength as a life jacket, holding me above the rough

waters.

I remember when my mom as in the hospital on the ventilator. That was such an awful time for me! I lived at the hospital. Tony took care of everything! I remember praying constantly. You may find this hard to believe, but my prayer was not to heal my mom. By this point, I knew that was unrealistic. My prayer was to take her peacefully. My prayer was also to help me make the right decision. Tony and I finally made the decision to stop the life support! I will tell you that making that decision was one of the most profound moments in my life. For those of you who have had to make that choice, you understand. It was a life changing moment. The night before we stopped the ventilator, Tony and I shared the most amazing few hours with my mother. The words we shared will stay with me forever. In and out of consciousness, she spoke to us. She tried to write a few times, but that didn't work well. Tony had a wonderful relationship with my mom. Believe me, they have had their moments; but he considered her special like his mother and for that, she was so proud. She told us how very proud she was of us. I cherish that now. I can honestly tell you, even though she recovered from that experience, when I said goodbye to her that evening, it really was goodbye. She was NEVER the same person again. I do believe God lent her to us for a short time. She was such a huge part of our lives in celebrating one of our boys' births. She was here for the birth of our fourth and final son not even a year after her being in the hospital and so close to death! God works in amazing ways, don't you think? I am so thankful for that evening, and I am beyond grateful for the extra time she was here. I am even thankful for the times we argued.

My mom loved cigarettes and food that was bad for her! I can tell you stories that will make you wet your pants from laughing. She was a riot! Sometimes, though, I wanted to choke her. Other times, all I could do was laugh!

Do you know how many times I would drive across town with a nice meal for her? You know what she would do? Throw it away! In the trash it went.

She'd say, "Let's order a pizza!" or "How about getting me a quarter pounder with cheese?" Real healthy, Mom! Who's the one with heart disease and has about one hundred pounds to shed?

Oh and how about the cigarettes! I just would not buy them for her. ABSOLUTELY NOT! She would get everyone else to buy them and curse me out each time! It was hysterical.

These are the things I think about when I need a quick laugh! She was not allowed to smoke in our home; so she would stand outside in the bitter cold in her bright orange bathrobe, and we would wave to her from the windows! I even got Tony and the boys in on the act. The neighbors probably thought we were loony! Well, we are a little!

God, my mom was funny; although I don't think most of it was intentional. I think we were sort of like Ralph Camden and Ed Norton. She would irritate me to no end. I could always really get her going and keep her going, for that matter!

I am so thankful for all those silly little fights. I am even thankful for all the fights that weren't so silly. I am thankful for every moment she was a part of my life. I will miss her each day for the rest of my life, but we had such a great time together. Until I see her again, I will continue to laugh, smile and cry with every memory!

# GOODBYE MOM

*I knew the day was coming*

*but how was I to prepare…*

*for the empty feeling left behind*

*knowing you are no longer here?*

*I think I can handle anything.*

*Believe me, I really do try.*

*The strength that has gotten me through,*

*was YOU always by my side.*

*I cannot believe that you're really gone!*

*Although, I know I will see you again.*

*The love that we shared was truly unique,*

*for that love, Mom, there will be no end!*

# Journal

3/09/04

Hi, there!

So many of you have been calling to see how we are doing and to ask about Nino that I thought I'd fill you in on the latest visit to NIH.

The neurologist was very reassuring. He saw no need for Nino to go through further testing with him. He feels that Nino has some concerns, but they seem to be related to his genetic disorder rather than being neurological. Praise God!

On Wednesday of last week, we spent practically the entire day at the hospital. We met with a Physical Therapist, an Occupational Therapist, and a Rehabilitation doctor, who was incredible! We also met with a Genetic Counselor and two Genetic Specialists. It was a busy but rewarding day! The results highlighted a couple of indicators that were related to a specific genetic disease, and it gave a few hints to the Genetic Specialists.

One of the many wonderful things about NIH is the team effort! They listen to every word we tell them. They truly care. We feel that Nino is in such good hands!

# Journal

*After consulting with Dr. Kastner the next day, he really stressed the importance of doing a chromosomal test that we haven't done before. We are awaiting those results and praying for answers.*

*We may actually have a diagnosis! Do you know that shyness and a speech impediment, which are both symptoms of which Nino has, are indicators of this genetic disorder?*

*All of the swollen lymph nodes that were found during the surgery point to this specific genetic disorder as well. The disease is called Mevalonic Kinase Deficiency Disorder. WOW! We will keep you posted.*

*Pray for answers.*

*How are we doing? I am not sure how to respond. Each day is harder. Reality is smacking me in the face, and that is tough! Tony is a Godsend! He has taken care of my mom's apartment. He has cleaned the entire thing! He has handled most of the phone calls. I have learned so much about him recently! You know, sometimes we take people in our lives for granted. We expect certain "things", certain behaviors. How fair is that to the other person? Most of our married life, I have viewed Tony as a husband and a father. My mother's death has helped me to see him as a MAN. The sacrifices he makes for me, the protection he offers me, the comfort he gives me, are* all wrapped up in the very special gift of Tony. I do not know how I would have handled this situation without his support. On Friday morning, there were five messages on my mom's answering machine from me; I was yelling at her to pick up the phone! Nino was having a terrible day, and I couldn't run over and check on her just because she didn't want to answer the phone! If only I knew.

Thursday evening, the night she died, I went to see <u>The Passion of the Christ</u> with my friend Robin. We went to a 10:00 PM showing. I didn't call my mom to say, "Goodnight," which I almost always do! I wish I could go back, but I cannot! I wish I could tell her one more time how great she is! I wish I could give her one more hug! I wish I could yell at her once more about her smoking! I cannot.

You see, friends, we can never go back. We always have to move forward. We MUST be the very best we can be. We MUST love as completely as we can, always. We MUST give one hundred percent of ourselves, always! Just a few weeks ago, my mom and I had a very serious conversation. She said it made her feel so good to see how much support we received on our journey. She wished she was feeling better so that she could do more. She was proud of how we were handling Nino's care. She was proud of how *strong we had become. I thought to myself, she's talking about how strong we have become. What about her? She was the pillar of strength!*

*For those of you who knew her, would you not agree that "fighter" is a good word to describe her? She was strong and brave! My dad died in a boating accident almost eleven years ago. I often wonder how she went through that. Her strength amazed me; it also infuriated me at times! I thank her for encouraging me to do my best, even when I didn't feel like it!*

*I will miss my parents every moment for the rest of my life, and I will strive to be the very best I can be, which I hope will make them proud!*

*As for our journey with Nino, my have we grown! That's what this is all about. God doesn't give you more than you can handle. Sometimes you just have to reach out to HIM. Trust in HIM and in yourself. Be the best you can be, and give all you can give!*

*I thank you all for your love and support.*

*Please continue to pray for Nino.*

*May God bless you and your families.*

*Fondly,*

*Lori*

# Journal

03/18/04

Hi, everyone.

It is late Thursday evening, and the house is quiet. Imagine that!

Nino has had several bad days. I think we are getting out of a "flare."

He has been running a fever and is very congested. He has been having some

leg pain, but not as much as he usually does. We are hoping that the new

dosage of medicine is making the difference.

We'll go back to the Pediatric Center on Monday for more antibiotics. They

love us! Nino is on so many medications; it is incredible! The antibiotics seem

to be making a difference because he really has not been complaining about

pain, nor is he stuffy or coughing. Yeah! The boys have been wonderful!

Nino started Speech Therapy through the Intermediate Unit and goes every

Thursday. He has done so well with his speech; you'd be amazed! I am really

proud of him. Our dear friend Maureen keeps the others while I take Nino.

They love going to Maureen's, and they love her! She has chickens, lots of

dirt, and "roaming area". What a place for the Todaro boys!

The other day when we went for a blood count, the NEW technician was

concerned that Nino was too young to sit without pulling his arm away.

My, was he surprised!

# Journal

YOU should see the huge bruise on Nino's chin he got when he jumped from the sixth step of the staircase. When I asked him why he would do something so insane, he replied, "'Cause I can!" Case closed, end of story! Each day my eyes are opened to the wonderful blessings in my life. Tonight I visited with a dear friend, who is the boys' piano teacher. She lost her thirteen-year-old son in a car accident. What an amazing lady she is! During our discussion, I couldn't help but think of bedtime each night. I read with my boys, tuck them in, kiss them (even though Vinny won't admit it), and tell them I love them "higher than the sky, deeper than the ocean, wider than the world", knowing that if I do not wake up to see morning, my boys will NEVER doubt for a second how much they were loved! My friend lost that honor. Who am I to feel sad that Nino is dealing with so much? I feel blessed to know her and to have learned so much from her.

You know, sometimes we question why things happen, especially to those we love. We need to look at these situations not as something bad happening to us, but as events that are building who we are. Our situation is not always easy, but it is our situation. We are not the same people we were before. We will never be those people again.

# Journal

*A few years ago when Nino first became ill, I wondered what would happen. I blamed everyone! I was bitter! Now, we have come so far in self-growth. I want to enjoy Nino on the good days, comfort him on bad days, and be content with him on the so-so days.*

*One thing I wanted to mention was that on the day we lost my dad, I asked God why He didn't give my dad cancer or a terminal illness so that I would have had time to say good-bye and had time to prepare.*

*My mom has been sick for years. When the phone call came about her death, I was totally unprepared! I still felt like I didn't have time to prepare. You do what you have to do. There is NO easy way to go through any of these experiences. You have to make the best of every situation. If you don't, how will you ever see the beautiful light at the end of the tunnel?*

*I have been wondering about people who do not have GOD in their lives! My peace with my parents comes from knowing I'm going to see them again. My peace with Nino comes from trusting that the Lord trusts me. He believes in me. He gave me this amazing child, knowing that come what may, I can and will do it.*

*Again, thank you for being so supportive. It is wonderful to share our story with you. I know that it makes a difference to someone.*

# *Journal*

*We're only here on earth for awhile. We should do our best, be our best, and*

*love completely.*

*Have a good evening.*

*Love,*

*Lori*

*P.S. Please remember the Boyd's Bear Bingo is next Sunday, March 28th.*

*There are still tickets available. Call or email me and let me know how many*

*tickets you need. Thanks so much!*


*3/28/04*

*Hello.*

*Someone mentioned to me today that they haven't received an update in*

*awhile, and they were concerned. I am glad that so many of you take the*

*time to read them and are part of this journey with us.*

*The last couple of weeks have been a little difficult.*

*Adjusting to life without my mom has been tough. I never realized what*

*an impact she had on my life. I never realized how much I depended on her,*

*emotionally and physically. I never dreamed I'd miss her so much!*

# Journal

It also has been a rough road for Nino. He has been hit really hard with two back-to-back flares. It really scared us! Last weekend, he had what seemed to be a flare with some respiratory stuff going on. He was feeling great on Tuesday, but Wednesday was one of the worst days we've had in awhile. We have had a tough time getting his fevers to stay down. His legs have been hurting, and he has been so tired. When he is having an episode, he gets very little sleep, which makes for a very unhappy young man! I am telling you, God has something truly amazing planned for this guy!

With all of this going on, Tony was at training most of the week. Thank God for Joey and Vinny. They are truly wonderful!

I recently had a conversation with a friend who is not a fan of home schooling. She questioned how "healthy" it is for the boys to witness so much pain and suffering! She also wondered how much information they are actually able to process. Hmmmmmm. I have thought a great deal about that conversation and would like to point out a couple of things.

I think pain and suffering are facts of life! I think all of us interpret information our own way. When I watch our boys, who are growing into men, comfort their hurting brother, hold Angelo and read to him, or give me a hug at a certain moment in my day, I think, what a blessing our boys are!

# Journal

*Life is not always easy. There are struggles each day; you don't give up or give in. You do your best, and you move forward. Trust in the Lord, and He will trust in you! I hope this home school experience is teaching the boys such life lessons as these!*

*I have some amazing news! Not only was today beautiful with the sun shining, birds singing, and ALL of our boys running and playing, but the Boyd's Bear Bingo was a HUGE SUCCESS! I could not believe the turnout. Wow! I was so moved that so many of you came out to support our family. What a difference you have made! God bless you all.*

*The hot tub is totally wired and ready to roll. Nino is so excited, and we are all excited for him!*

*One last thought I'd like to share is that last week after Mass, I had a wonderful talk with one of our priests. I told him that things were very difficult lately, and that I am having a tough time expressing myself to others. He gave me such valuable advice that I will never forget; therefore, I wanted to share it with you. He said, "Preach constantly, and use words only when necessary." That statement will stay in my heart forever.*

I should bring this to a close for tonight. I wanted to fill you in on the last couple of weeks. I also wanted to thank many of you for your support today, and thank all of you for your support each day.

Please be good to each other. Don't waste a single moment. Good or bad, make the most of it, and always be your best!

Thanks again. We are so blessed!

Fondly,

Lori


4/25/04

Good Evening.

It is Sunday evening, and it has been a busy weekend. Yesterday was the opening day of Baseball season for Joe. I am so very proud of him! His first game was incredible. The team played well; he played well, and he felt great about his efforts! He has grown so much this past year. Sometimes it amazes me to see how quickly the time has passed.

Nino is having a terrible time. Friday evening the boys stayed with Mrs. K, a teacher at Saint Patrick School. They had a great time, and so did she! It was the first evening since summer that Tony and I have been kid- free. I was in a state of disbelief. I must have checked their rooms a dozen times through the night!

By the time we got the boys home at 8:00 on Saturday morning, Nino was complaining. He was really tired, and all day today he has been having terrible stomach pain. We have been on the phone a couple of times with the doctor. We are trying a new medicine tonight, just to help him get through this pain. We will see where tomorrow takes us.

We are at Hershey on Wednesday and return to NIH next Monday. Unfortunately, the Enbrel, which was supposed to alleviate the fevers, joint pain, and flares, hasn't accomplished what we were hoping it would. Therefore, we will need to try a new treatment plan, which worries me a little. The METHOTREXATE has side effects, like stomach irritation and low energy, that I was thankful not to have experienced with the ENBREL. But, we have to do what we have to do.

Keep praying. It is difficult that these flares keep happening, and we are not able to stop them. As a mom, I feel that I am supposed to protect my children, keep them safe, and keep them comfortable. I am not always able to do that for Nino, and that breaks my heart.

# Journal

I haven't sent an update in some time. I think sometimes that you must get tired of hearing that we have been experiencing another tough time. This is not easy folks! I do try to always mention how much my faith is getting me through. That is a fact! Sometimes though, I don't think you realize how difficult some days are. I would wish this on no one! I personally have grown so much through this experience that I would never want to go back to the person I was before. That in NO WAY means I wouldn't want to change what Nino has endured.

I am missing my mom more and more each day. I miss being able to call her when all I want to do is cry. I miss just being able to ask her to sit with the others while I run Nino up to the hospital for blood work. I miss being able to have her tell me on a bad day that I am doing a good job. Don't take any moment in your life for granted friends.

I am sad tonight. Sometimes no matter how hard you try, you just cannot fix everything. I continue to pray for Nino. I continue to pray for myself as a mom. I continue to pray that our family be strengthened by this journey.

As always, I continue to pray for all of you. I pray that God may touch your hearts and your lives. Please remember that who you are is your gift from God, what you make of yourself is your gift back to Him!

*Peace and Blessings to you.*

*Love,*

*Lori*

*4/28/04*

*Hello!*

*Our Hershey appointment went well today. The blood work was fine. Nino has some discomfort and stiffness in his hips and groin. He was very exact in showing Dr. Groh where his pain is and how badly it hurts. Dr. Groh and I talked about our next visit to NIH, as well as the test results.*

*It seems as though we are on to something. Everything is definitely related, and we trust that we will soon name the gene that is the defect! Keep praying. After all, prayers are the best medicine!*

*We received wonderful news the other day. A director from the Children's Inn called and asked if we would be the poster family for the Inn. What an honor! Next week, the Inn is celebrating the opening of the new wing. Just think how many families benefit from this place. It is incredible! The best word I can use to describe my feeling is HUMBLED. That is truly how I feel each time I journey to the Inn. Everyone at the Inn, the many faces, the* many cultures, the many faiths, is one big FAMILY. It is just amazing, and we are so honored! Wednesday evening will be the opening ceremony. Our family will tell our story and the difference the Inn makes in our lives! The boys will also have a portrait taken for the brochures. Isn't this cool?

The boys and I are reading ISLAND and are at a really interesting part, so I will end the email for now.

I will keep you informed of our NIH visit and the new treatment plan.

Many blessings to all of you. You continue to be in our thoughts and prayers. God bless.

Fondly,

Lori

5/07/04

Hi, there!

We just arrived home tonight, and we are exhausted! Our appointments at the hospital took ALL day! Our first appointment was scheduled for 9:00 AM, and we left the hospital at 3:00 this afternoon. We didn't even have time for lunch! Nino had graham crackers and apple juice on the run.

# Journal

We did hear lots of information. We will begin a new treatment, HUMIRA,

in about seven weeks. HUMIRA is a TNF (tumor necrosis factor) inhibitor.

You see, Nino's immune system doesn't "work" the way it should; it

doesn't turn on and off when fighting off infection. Nino's immune system

continuously fights, thinking there is always an infection. This is important

to understanding his condition. We know what his body is doing, we know

the symptoms he has, but we don't know the gene causing the defect. Do

you understand? TNTs are little "things" that "float" throughout your body

when you are sick. The receptors on the end of each TNF come out, fight

the infection, break off, and dissolve. Nino's little receptors are always

present. This is NOT a good thing because if it has nothing to fight as far

as infection, it begins to fight "good" things, like organs and tissues, in his

body. We cannot have that, which is why Nino is taking a medication to

suppress his immune system. Dr. Groh referred to his immune system as

"hyperactive", which should help you understand!

Well, the new medications that we discussed today because the Enbrel is

helping slightly but NOT enough, are Remicade and Humira. Tony and I,

as well as the geneticist, thought Nino should take the HUMIRA. It is a

subcutaneous injection given several times a week, which is what we are *doing with the Enbrel. Remicade is a weekly infusion which is done in the hospital. Both treatments are TNF Inhibitors.*

*I hope you understand all of this. I don't think I am able to explain in words what I understand the doctors saying to me, but trust in us because we think we are doing what is best for Nino!*

*There were a few other concerns discussed, specifically stomach problems. We are praying that Nino doesn't need a surgical procedure to remove the mass of lymph nodes that were found in his colon, which is what we will find out during our return visit to NIH in seven weeks. In the meantime, we have increased the Enbrel dose to its MAX. We will continue with the Enbrel for the next seven weeks until more test results are back. When we return, we will begin the Humira and have a set plan for Nino's stomach problems.*

*Next we discussed Nino's feet and hips! He had many x-rays today. He is so brave! There have been inflammation and swelling in his feet and hips in the last few weeks; we will know the x-ray results in the next couple of days. We do not want any sign of joint destruction, so please keep praying! The orthopedic department can make incredible inserts for Nino's Birkenstock sandals! Nino said they are so comfy! He is having such a hard time wearing anything that encloses his foot; it is really a problem. As much as he loves* soccer, he has even asked not to go to practice or games because he doesn't want to put on his soccer socks and cleats because it hurts too much! We are working on it!

Well, let me tell you about the INN. WOW! The opening ceremonies were amazing! The reception was beautiful! We were so honored to be a part of the festivities. Our family was interviewed by a writer for "The Washington Post". The story will be in next Thursday's edition! There were so many media there, so keep a look out! All of the INN children, including all of our boys, were invited to go on stage for the ribbon cutting; it was so moving! They added twenty-two new rooms, several more activity rooms, and an entire dining area. What a miracle this place is in our lives! We of course met several families on this visit. One, in particular, had a seven-month-old son named Joseph. The parents stopped and talked to us as we were eating dinner, and then asked if they could pray with us. They are a beautiful family and will forever be in our prayers.

Our friend Dixie took care of Rexx and Lola. I hear they had a great time. I know Dixie did!

Things are going well for us. We are wrapping up our school year and are very excited about that! What a year it has been.

*Tony had an awesome arrest the other day, and the boys and I are so proud of him! We are family, guys! It is NOT always easy, but it is our commitment to each other and our love for each other that makes us really appreciate all that we have! Reach out to others; let them know how much they mean to you. Life is an amazing journey, but you never go back; you are always moving forward. Make the most of it!*

*This week has been full of emotion; please continue to pray for Nino. We will continue to trust in the Lord, the wonderful medical professionals, and in ourselves! I don't know what God's plan is for our life, but I keep moving ahead one moment at a time! May God bless you and your families.*

*Fondly,*

*Lori and Tony*

*P. S. If you know of anyone selling a used double jogging stroller, PLEASE pass our name and number along. We are having a tough time carrying Nino when he is unable to get around, but a regular double stroller will not hold the weight! Please let us know if you hear of anything! Thanks so much!*

# *Journal*

Well, Happy Mother's Day to all of my friends who are amazing Moms and who inspire me daily!

Nino has been feeling well, and our Mother's Day was beautiful. Our boys used their "own money" to buy me a candle and flowers. It was awesome! My mother-in-law came for dinner, and we had a very nice visit. I prepared a big dinner, which kept me very busy! I must have mentioned my mom a billion times. For those of you who are blessed to still have your moms, I hope you told them how much they mean to you. When my mom died, the one thing I was most grateful for was that she knew how much I loved her! Well, enough of the tears.

I hope you are well. The weather is beautiful. You can never have enough sunshine!

I DID receive a wonderful gift yesterday from a friend. My dear friend Mary called and said she was dropping off a double jogging stroller! She has four children and doesn't use it anymore. What a gift!

On really bad days, we could use a wheelchair; but we have chosen not to do so. We do not feel that is an option! I WILL NOT use one until I have no other choice. I want Nino to push himself as hard as he can. To me, a wheelchair would be too easy!

We have a week off before we return to Hershey Medical Center, and May 17th we return to Lancaster to see the gastroenterologist. We are praying that surgery will not be necessary, but it seems to be leaning that way. We will keep you posted.

Please make the most of everyday. We are only here for awhile, so we must live life to the fullest. Make someone smile today; tell someone how "cool" you think they are. Maybe the life you touch today will make ALL the difference.

God bless you all. Thanks for sharing this journey with us.

Fondly,

Lori


5/13/04

Hi!

Every year on May 13th I would wake up to my mom screaming, "Happy Birthday". Today, it really hit home when I awoke and didn't hear my mom. The silence quickly reminded me that she is not here to say that anymore. I have been thinking about past birthdays and how very special they were,

but today was just as special! Tony had a beautiful cake and cards waiting

for me this morning. My dear friend Andrea prepared dinner and brought

over a cake for the boys to decorate. Maureen and the boys designed the most

beautiful birthday banner. Stephanie and the kids called first thing this

morning to sing, "Happy Birthday". Thanks, everyone!

My mom is not here physically, but she is here in spirit!

I am so excited to share all of my happy birthday memories with the boys. It

is a beautiful day, the sun is shining, the birds are singing, and ALL the boys

are running and playing. Today is definitely a beautiful day!

That is it, folks.

Cherish all the moments you have.

Be ever thankful for all of your blessings.

God bless you!

Lori


5/18/04

Good Morning!

Yesterday, Nino had a visit with the gastroenterologist, and I was pretty nervous. Currently, the team from NIH and the gastroenterologist are trying

to determine a solution for all of Nino's stomach and bowel problems. It

is truly upsetting me! Nino has been taking laxatives for awhile now, but

they do not help! He is sometimes so uncomfortable; it is a shame. After all

of the testing, his condition has been labeled "irritable bowel syndrome".

I don't really care what they call it; I just want to know how it can be

fixed! Unfortunately, with his disease, this is a condition that develops.

My prayer for the last few weeks, since our return from NIH, has been for

Nino NOT to have another surgery. After our visit yesterday, there is still no

determination; but the gastroenterologist suggested Nino be put on a high

fiber diet. He also added another medication to help with comfort, as well

as a fiber supplement. The laxative works independently; but when mixed

with the pain medication (Tylenol with Codeine) that Nino takes frequently

for pain, it really isn't able to do anything! We are not able to stop the pain

medicine, so we are going to try to work around it. As of right now, NO

surgery is set or recommended; we have to wait to hear from NIH regarding

the test results. PLEASE keep praying.

For those of you who called last night, thank you! I am so blessed that so

many of you really care. Mitzi, thanks for getting the number for me.

# Journal

Last night I was so exhausted; I truly had myself so worked up. I wanted

to send an update, and I got distracted. I sat down after the boys went

to sleep and was flipping through the channels. I came across a show on

HBO. It was more of a documentary, sort of like a reality show. The story

was about a woman named Susan Tom who had thirteen children. Eleven

of her children were special needs children, and they were adopted. The

story spanned several days, months, and seasons. Tony kept saying, "Are

you crying? Are you okay?" I was so inspired by this woman! Some days

I think, how can I juggle all of Nino's medications and therapies? When

Nino is experiencing pain, I ask God to give me more strength! This woman

was so amazing. She took care of all of the children with incredible grace

and compassion. During the months of taping, two of her children died. She

continued to love and support unconditionally. It was truly amazing. Again,

my life was blessed; my heart was humbled.

Years ago the focus in my life was so different than it is today. I am such a

better person because of this experience. I wish that all of us could be blessed

with a truly humbling experience; it really teaches the value of life, and the

appreciation that words cannot describe.

# Journal

Sometimes after speech therapy, Nino and I go over to the McDonald's Playland and have some time together. Although the other day was a "bad" day for him, we decided to go to lunch at McDonald's for his favorite, french fries and a vanilla shake; and he could play in the small ball pit! I overheard two women that I knew, one with five children and one with two and pregnant, discussing their day; and it was only 11:30 in the morning. They were complaining about the kids getting up so early, their having so much laundry to do, the baby teething and staying up all night, the check-out line at Giant being so long and the kids being so restless, etc.... Meanwhile, I am sitting there watching Nino playing at the table because his legs hurt too badly to go and run around Playland! Finally one mom screamed at her daughter, "Go play and leave me alone!" That was it! I should have kept it together, but I couldn't! I simply cleaned off the table and politely said, "If you were in my shoes, you'd love the opportunity to stop your griping and enjoy your children playing!"

You know, friends; life is such an incredible gift! Why waste a single moment? Why complain about the little things that may not go your way? LOOK AROUND YOU! What an incredible life we lead. Be thankful for all you are and have.

# Journal

Thanks for sharing our journey. Thanks again for all of you who care so much. Your calls really touched my heart last night. Many of you knew how upset I was yesterday, and you really cared. Thanks! Kathy, thank you very specially for our conversation.

May God bless you all. You continue to be in our prayers.

Fondly,

Lori


5-20-04

Hi, there.

Believe it or not, ALL of the boys are still asleep!

Our school year finished up last week, and they love it!

Last week Nino suffered another seizure and had a pretty mild flare for a few days. In the midst of all of this, his toes were killing him. His feet have been a problem for a couple of years, and they are getting worse. Well, Tuesday morning he cried all morning asking me, "Can Dr. Holly cut off my toes?" I realized what he was saying when I checked out his toes closely and found that one of his toenails was (and still is) actually lifted from the nail bed and was bleeding. I also noticed a few other nails were cracked across the center and lifting; they just weren't as bad, yet! I have learned so much

about this condition in the last two days that I should write a book. It is

a very uncomfortable and painful condition that develops in people with

psoriatic arthritis, which is what gave the doctors the idea to test for this

disease during our last visit to NIH. The pediatrician suggested that we go

to another specialist. No wonder his feet are such a sore place for him. The

advice by the arthritis foundation is NOT to remove the nail. However, we

can't just leave it there.

I cannot even imagine what he endures daily. I am so inspired by him. His

love of life is unreal. He is such an incredible little boy. When you see him on

good days you would just find it hard to believe.

Today we are seeing a Pediatric Podiatrist. The earliest appointment time

I could get with the Pediatric Dermatologist is next Wednesday. Today is

Speech at 10:00, and the podiatrist appointment is at 12:30.

I spoke for awhile last night with a good friend who is also Nino's pediatrician.

She really shed a bright light on the whole situation. You know, all of these

things that are happening with Nino (belly problems, enlarged lymph nodes in his

colon, reflux, speech delay, joint swelling, redness, and nail growth deformities)

are all pieces to the big puzzle. These things are not easy to deal with time and time again. I don't know how Nino stays so positive. Each and every day wonderful things are happening in our lives. Looking back I am so overwhelmed by how far we have come. Last year in May he was in the hospital again, and we were praying to be accepted to NIH. Although the medication isn't taking away the flares, it is giving him reprieve during non-flares.

He is just a little boy. God has been SO good to us. Please pray that the specialists are able to help with the pain and discomfort. I am not a fool, folks. I know they cannot make everything all better. They can help with pain management, but the rest is in God's hands! Believe me; I am using every grace that God has given me to be Nino's biggest advocate. Sometimes I wish I had a little more self-control, as it is a little frustrating sometimes. I want/need the doctors to listen to me. For the most part, they do! He is my amazing gift from God, and I will do whatever I have to do!

So, we're off again to doctors for most of the day. Please continue to pray, and I will try to keep you posted!

May you have a blessed day. It is cloudy out this morning; but you'll find the sunshine, if you just keep looking for it.

Love,

Lori

# Journal

It's another day, and there's another doctor visit. We visited a specialist in Hershey today. I won't mention names or specialty because I was very unhappy! I have so much respect and admiration for the medical professionals caring for Nino, but today was a bummer! We actually had a couple of appointments that took most of the day. Friends were kind enough to bring dinner over. Thank you! You have NO idea what a huge help that is.

Maureen took Joe, Vinny, and Angelo on a hike; and they ALL had a blast. Let me share some of my feelings about the first visit this morning. The doctor was very professional. She did not listen to Nino or me; she spoke at us and not to us. As far as I'm concerned, that's a no-no! You see, we have come too far in this journey not to keep the big picture in mind. Right now, I don't care about all the technical terms; all I care about is keeping my son comfortable! Can you understand? She had a few interesting points, and some not so interesting ones; so I called Tony at work, and we decided to get another opinion.

We have to trust ourselves above all. Remember, I always say that you can never go back. We must keep moving forward. I find it funny to hear people complaining about situations in their lives. If you are not being the best you can be or if you are preventing others from being the best they can be, stop your whining and do something about it! Sorry if that sounds mean, but why waste so much time! Let me get on my "soap-box" for a moment.

Twice today I fell apart thinking of my mom. Why today? Who knows! Both times Nino and I were in the Hershey Medical Center cafeteria. While in line paying, a young mom with a quite ill little boy in a stroller called to her mom to please grab a diet Pepsi for her. That was too close to home, as that is something that I would ask my mom to do. After regrouping, we entered the dining area to sit down. Nino, proud as all get out, had his Cheerios and milk. A young couple was cooing over their brand new baby. Guess who was holding the baby? Yes, Grandmom! It was a rough day, emotionally, for me.

Nino is feeling well. He had some belly problems over the weekend, but we are sure it was medicine related.

The boys are doing so well. Vinny is trying out for the Fall Soccer traveling team. He is so young, but he wanted to give it a try; and we are so proud of him! Joe has the absolute best heart! He is a gem. Angelo is such a flirt. Goodness. He simply has a sweet disposition and a love of life. He is such a gift for us. Then there is Nino. WOW! He is going to give his Kindergarten teacher a run for her money! He is such a little comedian. My mom always told me that I let him get away with too much and he is paying us back. I say, "Go for it, buddy! You've earned the right to act up, sometimes!" And, of course, there's Tony. What a guy! He is so admirable and strong.

I haven't been myself for a few days. I really don't like seeing my son suffer. I try my best to help with comfort, and it is sad when I cannot. His feet have really been bothering him, and it just seems like its one more thing. Tony has been working a lot of hours, and my mom is not here. I am a little down. I have faith and hope more now than ever, but there are sad days! A very special friend of mine gave me a gift of my favorite perfume today. How cool was that! What a thoughtful thing to do. We are so blessed in our lives. I want to bring this to a close, but before I do I really want to point something out. Many of you have been so kind to us. You will never know how much it is appreciated! Sometimes I think twice about sending an update. You see, this is our life. As far as we know, this will be our life forever. We have amazing days, we have so-so days, and we have bad days. We make the most of each day we have. My wish for all of you is that you make the most of each day that you have. Look around you; say a *little prayer of thanks. We are ALL so very blessed. Please remember that*

*blessings come in many shapes and sizes. Take care. God bless.*

*Love,*

*Lori*

There are times when I think I am not able to make it across the next river, lake, or stream. Ahead of me, I see a bridge guiding me across. Tony is the strong solid aid that is protecting me from the waters.

Marriage is hard work!

While on this journey, I have learned a lot about my partner. It is very easy to walk away, and it is hard to stay and make a marriage work. The statistic is very high for marriages to fail when couples are faced with a chronically or terminally ill child. Why is that? No other person on this earth loves our child more than we do. We have that common bond. You know what, though? It's easier to turn inward and turn away from the pain, rather than turn to trust in your spouse. It hurts! It's tough! The reward of a committed love far outweighs the pain from tragedy and despair! The experiences Tony and I have faced in our marriage have been incredible! Either of us could have thrown in the towel, and we have thought about it! When the storm got rocky, we were there for each other! We always have been. You grow in marriage. That fuzzy, young love develops into something deeper. The glance he gives me to say he understands, the look he gives me when the doctor is saying something that I don't want to hear, his strong supportive arms around me when I lost my parents, the love and guidance he gives to our boys, the committed support he gives to me, are all what our marriage is about. I think being a spouse is the hardest job in the world. I think it's even harder than parenting, but I also think it's the most rewarding! You see, the boys are watching everything we do. They learn their ways through us. They are building their lives. I pray our boys will one day be kind fathers and loving husbands, just like Tony. Tony and I have together made these beautiful children, and an amazing legacy!

# Journal

*5/29/04*

I just logged on to check my email for the day and felt the need to share.

This evening I had a nice talk with someone I really look up to, one of

our priests. He gave me a refreshing perspective. A word that he used was

"surrender". How appropriate! I don't think I have ever thought of our

situation quite that way. I am unable to micro-manage everything and

everyone. That is a given; but, if I just surrender it all to the Lord and do

the very best I can, how can I fail? This is not about anyone or anything

else. This is simply the plan God has for us and where it leads. He will

follow. I am just a vessel on the journey. There are so many details of which

to keep track: medications, charts, fevers, appointments, insurance, real

life schedules, etc... If I realize that I am not the one in control, I will go

bonkers; however I know I'll be okay with God in control.

Nino had Kindergarten "fly-up" yesterday. It was so cool! I was very

worried about how he would do, but he did great! I got to talk with some

friends who were also there with their children. It was a good feeling to

know that we were all so typical. It was a good day for him. He was so

excited! Of course, I cried. Just eight months ago we didn't know where we'd be right now! Whenever we make it to the next step, I feel as though I've jumped across a river and landed safely on the other side.

There are still several things happening. We are consulting with an Orthopedic Surgeon about Nino's toenails. We are anxious to get the test results back from NIH on June 30th. We are deciding what to do about his belly issues. These are a foreword to a wonderful summer.

Hopefully toward the end of the summer we will journey to New Jersey to place my mom's ashes with my dad's, which will be a proud moment for both Tony and me. Since they did so much for us, we will have peace and confidence knowing we are able to do this for them!

I continue to keep all of you in our prayers. You are such blessings in our lives. I am going to continue to work on surrendering my "control" to the Lord, trusting that He is the only one in control; and I pray that you will do the same.

Have a good evening. Have a great holiday weekend. Enjoy yourself, and have fun!

Fondly,

Lori

# Journal

Hello.

I hope this message finds you well. We are doing okay. We are keeping as busy as ever, to which I'm sure you can relate.

The boys were so excited to attend St. Patrick School's Fly-up Day. They met with their new teachers and got to see old friends. They are really excited to be returning. I am very happy that Nino did so well with Kindergarten fly-up and screening.

He has been very tired and has looked really pale for the last week, which actually has me more concerned than his joint pain. I guess what I can't see concerns me more than what I can see. Usually we can manage his pain in his legs and feet because it is more physical. When other things are going on with his high blood counts, the bleeding ulcers, or things of that nature, it is internal and can be very serious! We worry because we can't see it.

Tuesday morning at 7:00 we have an appointment with the Orthopedic Surgeon. We really respect this doctor. He has worked with Nino since the beginning. We will discuss Nino's toenails with him and decide whether or not they will be surgically removed. We will keep you posted!

# Journal

On Friday of this week we are back to Hershey Medical Center for a follow-up visit, and I am sure more laboratory tests will be ordered, as I have a concern that Nino is bruising so badly. Right now it's a concern of mine, but I will address it with the doctor!

Well, I wanted to share an update and keep you posted. Your prayers continue to support us. Your kindness continues to touch our lives.

On a bright note, Thursday evening the boys will have their piano recital. Yeah! I wish I knew how to play; I think piano music is so beautiful! I also think it is pretty cool to see a man playing the piano! I am really looking forward to it. Each year the recital is held close to or on my mom's birthday, and she always looked forward to the big event. After the recital she always took the boys for sundaes to celebrate. I know she will be watching this year, too!

By any chance does anyone have copies of past updates? We have been working with a publisher and an illustrator and are very excited about this book project! However, I passed several of the updates on to friends, and they were misplaced. I do not have copies! I am somewhat desperate for any past updates anyone can gather. I tried to retrieve them from my computer, and they are permanently deleted. PLEASE let me know as soon as you can

if you have any. Thanks!

Steph and Denay, thanks for all your help with the copies.

Be kind to one another. Keep trusting in God for all things!

God Bless,

Lori


6/17/04

Hello.

In the last couple of days, three people have emailed me or have mentioned to

me in person that they haven't seen an update in awhile. Knowing that so

many of you care so much really warms my heart! Thank you!

Well, it has been just about five weeks since Nino's last flare. That is

awesome! Our pediatrician has been keeping a close eye on Nino's blood

work. He has been tiring easily, and he has a cut that is not healing well.

He has also been very pale and cranky, so Dr. Holly is really keeping a close

watch.

During our last visit to NIH the doctors increased his ENBREL dose to

the maximum amount. Up to that point, he wasn't really showing much improvement. Maybe the increased dose is doing the trick. However,

we cannot have things go crazy with his counts or anemia due to the

medications. Nino also caught Angelo's cold, and it has him bummed. Keep

positive, though. So far, so good!

We couldn't go to the pool today, because it rained. The boys, of course, say

they are bored; but I can certainly find a dozen things to occupy them!

I have been busy working with Dr. Laws critiquing the book, and I am

so excited. The illustrator is working on his end, and I cannot wait to

see his work! All things happen for a reason. The project is really coming

together, and I am praying it will touch at least one person's life! If God

brings you to it, He will bring you through it! Keep the faith, my friends!

Tomorrow would have been my mom's 59th birthday. WOW! It is still hard

to believe she is gone! I talk to her all the time. Angelo says "Mom-Mom" all

the time. I keep trying to teach him to say "Heaven", and it sounds like he's

trying! The boys and I are going to bake a cake, and we are trying to firm up

plans for our journey to New Jersey to bury my mom with my dad.

I hope you are enjoying your summer so far. It is my favorite time of year!

Our return to NIH is scheduled for June 30th. Our friend Theresa has

offered to keep the boys. Tony and I will get a lot of information at this next visit because we are supposed to begin the new treatment. We think it's

important for both of us to meet with the doctors. The boys are really looking

forward to hanging out with Mrs. K, as she will be Vinny's second grade

teacher.

Of course, we will keep you posted on what we learn at NIH. Thanks for

your support and prayers.

I pray you are all well.

Take care of yourselves and please be good to each other!

Love,

Lori

# Journal

*6/30/04*

*Hello!*

*I am writing from the Inn. We had a great visit today. Nino has been doing very well these last few weeks. The Rehabilitation doctors do not need to see him again for awhile, which is awesome! Unless he has a pretty serious flare, we are actually "dismissed" from rehab treatment, which is great!*

*The next progression is to get Nino back into shoes and sneakers. For about the last six months, he hasn't been able to tolerate closed shoes or socks on his feet, specifically rubbing against his toes. Since he has not been having flares (swelling), his feet are not as sensitive; so the transition begins.*

*As I am sitting here in the computer room typing, two teenage patients, a girl and a boy, are having a cool discussion. The girl said, "Hi, what's your name?" He replied with his name and said, "What's yours?" She replied with her name and her disease. He then, of course, filled her in about his condition. She has a brain tumor, and he has a rare white blood cell disease. It completely blows my mind that this place is so incredible. Our boys at home discuss what new video game is out, who's sleeping over, what movie they want to see, etc.; and the children at the Inn are discussing their conditions as a matter of fact, just as my boys have the other discussions at* home. You get the idea! The environment here is so positive, but there is a sense of lost innocence. We can only admire and appreciate the gifts these kids have to offer because we can never fully understand where they are.

Well, again I felt the need to share. I am so inspired each time we visit the Inn, and humbled! I wish I could bring all of you with us to one visit at the Children's Inn; you would NOT believe it. What a blessing this place is in our lives.

Tony and I are a little worried about our visit with genetics in the morning. The suggestion at our last visit was to change the medication this time. However, since that visit, when they increased the dose of Enbrel, Nino has been free of flares! That is definitely reason to rejoice. We will stress this to the doctors tomorrow and hope that they will agree with our plan to continue the Enbrel for a few more weeks to see if it continues to make such a difference.

We are also scheduled to see an audiologist. Nino has some hearing loss in his right ear, which is something new; we are not sure if it is related to his medicines or his disease, so we will meet with that department tomorrow as well. We will continue to keep you posted.

Please keep praying; it really makes all the difference. Prayer for me has been such a calming effect, as well as my writing. I wonder sometimes how people handle hard times without prayer. It gives me an inner peace to know that I offer my worries up to the Lord and that I really let it go. There is not much that I have control over in this situation. I just do the very best I can, offer the rest up to Him, and live life. My writing has given me a way to express myself and again let it go. I get it off my chest and move on to the next thing.

I spoke to the boys tonight before they went to bed. They are staying with Mrs. K back at home. They are having a blast; and, of course, they are a huge help with Angelo. Nino is bummed that the boys often get to do fun things while he is away; it does have to be disappointing for him. I am very proud of my boys. They seem so normal through it all, and yet so sensitive. I am really honored to be their mom.

I am working on a fundraiser to benefit The Children's Inn. Mark your calendars for September 12th! The Boiling Springs Pool has generously donated the pool for the day. We will have a cook-out lunch, and we are working on getting some special guests to attend. Reserve your spot today. This gives you plenty of time to plan ahead if you live out of town! We are going to have an amazing time, and what a great cause. Adult tickets are

$10, kids are $5, and children under 2 are free. I'm sure that everyone will have fun, fun, fun!

Well, I should bring this to a close for tonight. I was so excited to tell you about Nino's great news today! We just jumped across another lake, and I feel the land beneath me!

Thanks to all of you for everything! Your thoughts and prayers and kind words really touch my heart. Remember to tell those around you how important they are. Remember to count your blessings and have tons of fun!

Peace and Love.

Fondly,

Lori


7/01/04

Hello everyone.

We arrived home from the Inn tonight. It was a good visit with a lot of hope! It was decided that Nino will remain on Enbrel until our next visit, which is in seven weeks. Since we have been seeing a big improvement in Nino's health the last few weeks, the doctors really want to give the Enbrel a chance. Nino's knee had some swelling, so he had to have some knee x-rays.

# Journal

The appointment with the audiologist went pretty well; there was a slight hearing loss found in his right ear, so he will be tested again when we return to the hospital in August. The results from the two tests will be compared, and then we will develop a plan. All of this is so promising.

I really hope my excitement and feeling of hope is coming across! It has been wonderful to have Nino almost pain-free these last few weeks. What an incredible perspective this little boy has given me!

I was SO happy to see the boys! You should have seen the great big smile Angelo gave me when he saw me. What a great feeling! Joe and Vinny were just as happy; and even though sometimes they think they're too cool to hug their mom in front of their friends, they did tonight! I hope they are getting the idea that the coolest thing in the world is to let others feel loved and important.

Nino's return visit to NIH is on his birthday. What a bummer! We are going to make it great, though! I am going to have Mr. Kilmore make the coolest cake with loads of ice cream, and decorate with streamers, etc... I know it's a long drive; but if anyone would be interested in checking out the Inn, this would be a great time! With all the sunshine this place has brought into our lives, what could be better than having a little celebration there!

# Journal

Well, I wanted to fill you in about today's appointments. It is late; and I am tired, but very glad to be home.

I told you all, never, ever lose hope!

Goodnight.

Love,

Lori


7/15/04

Hello.

I feel like it has been years since I've sent an update!

Things have been going rather well, and today was a big day. Nino was fitted for a pair of running shoes! This is reason to celebrate because since the end of February he has only been able to wear open-toed sandals. The shoes will be ready tomorrow afternoon because they had to build in the orthopedic insole. Yea!

Nino has been in rare form for the last few days, which is an understatement. It has been storming here, and the boys have had friends over. Well, look out, because Nino has been a wild man!

# Journal

*He was not feeling great on Sunday night and Monday; however, we spent the whole day on Sunday at DelGrosso's Amusement Park in Tipton, Pennsylvania, celebrating our niece's birthday. It was a great time, and the boys had so much fun. Nino didn't ride a lot of rides; he almost seemed "guarded". I am not sure how else to describe it. Even when he was trying shoes on today, he seemed so protective, as if he is expecting something to hurt.*

*Nino is currently taking Indocin, an anti-inflammatory medication, for a few days to help with comfort. Like I said, "He's a wild man!"*

*How are all of you?*

*Summer is such a busy time for everyone that we sometimes lose touch! We keep all of you in our thoughts and prayers and continue to thank you for all you do! I hope the summer is awesome for you. We are having a good time at the pool and enjoying family time. I have been really busy finishing up the book and am just about ready to send it to the publisher! The illustrator will have the pictures completed by the end of the month. Then, believe it or not, it's complete! It is truly amazing how the whole project just came together. Marc, thanks for the inspiration!*

# Journal

I have been thinking a lot about my parents lately and wondering what their thoughts would be about this whole book endeavor. God, I miss them so much! For example, today when I went to Dutrey's to have Nino sized for his shoes, I missed my mom. My mom always came along; she would hold Angelo and usually would read with the others while I took care of Nino. It's the little things, you know!

The other day, I heard a song (Would you guess I'm a country fan?) sung by Tim McGraw called, "Live Like You Were Dying". WOW! Whether you like country music or not, if you haven't heard this song before, you've got to listen to it. The words say everything I've been saying regarding this last year. Don't waste a moment! What if you were not here tomorrow? Would those around you know how much they mean to you? Were you unkind to someone to whom you can never apologize? Did you hug your kids, spouse or even your pet before you left for work? It all makes such a difference folks! Well, I guess that's enough preaching. I have really missed sending out an update, and I just wanted to let you know how things are going!

If you remember from our last update, Nino will be at the hospital for his sixth birthday; and Mr. Kilmore is making Nino a special cake for us to take to the hospital. We are going to make it the best birthday Nino has had yet.

Remember, if you are not too far away and want to come to the Inn for cake and ice cream, just let me know! Nino deserves a wonderful birthday. He has experienced so much this last year, and so have the other boys. We are going to PARTY!

Take care of yourselves and each other. I am so proud to know all of you and blessed to call you friends.

Fondly,

Lori


8/11/04

Hello friends.

We are home from vacation a day early because Nino is sick! His fever was 105 by the time we arrived back at the hotel last night, and this morning he was having a lot of joint pain and was vomiting. Joe had a headache and is stuffy, so here we are.

It was an amazing time, but it is always wonderful to come home. The boys loved the beach; they spent almost every moment on their boogie boards, and Nino was right there with them. Angelo liked the ocean; but he liked the sand and his buckets better.

# Journal

Tony and I had a great time with my cousin Donna, and she loved watching the boys play at the beach. Joe, the boys' Godfather, had a super time with us at the Great Adventure Safari and enjoyed spending time with the boys. We were able to see a great friend Susan and her daughters. We haven't seen them in about eight years, and it was so nice to visit with them. I actually took care of the girls when I was in college and was their gymnastics instructor. Now they are 19 and 20; Michele is studying education, and Diane is off to medical school. How cool is that? To be honest, though, it made us feel a little old. Susan spent time with us at the hotel and kept laughing while the boys jumped in and out of the water and chased each other around the pool. We must look like a circus act with four boys running wild, but I wouldn't change it for anything! We had dinner with my cousin Marc and his family on Tuesday, and it was awesome! Marc and I haven't seen each other since my dad died, so we had a lot of catching up to do. Marc's mom, my Aunt Honey, was not able to join us; but we hope to get together with them again very soon. My Aunt Honey was an incredible influence in my life, and I am really looking forward to her getting to know our boys.

# Journal

Nino has been having a lot of stomach problems the last several weeks. This morning it was really bad. The worst part about his situation is that we want to help him so badly, but we just cannot! Tony rubbed his back and held him in the hotel, and then it was my turn. Finally, after we cleaned up the mess of vomit, packed up, and checked out of the hotel, he said he was "starving"! We went to my parents' favorite diner for breakfast before we got on the road. As soon as we sat down, he got sick again! We did eventually get some breakfast, which he was able to keep down. We were finally on the road! Joe, Nino, and Angelo slept almost the whole way home; and Vinny read and played his Game Boy, how typical!

We are so glad that we went away. We had such a GREAT time; but while we were there we decided to take a drive by my parents' home. As we were driving down the road, we realized that the house was completely gone! Nothing but land and trees remained; it was a sad moment for me. It was almost as if they were gone, and nothing was left of them. After I thought about it and really thought clearly, I realized how silly that seems. The house was just a foundation, which crumbles and falls. The memories of my parents are alive in anyone who had the honor to know them. Tony and I, and our commitment to each other and to the boys, are all a part of my parents' legacy. I look at my boys and see my dad's smile. I ask Angelo, "Who loves you?" He replies, "Mom-Mom!" That's what it's all about. The house was just a building.

I haven't been back to my childhood home in almost eight years; and right across from my parents' land is a view of the river where my dad drowned. Looking at the river was VERY difficult for me; I pointed out the area to the boys and saw tears in Joe's eyes. I think the tears were for what he's missed more than for what the river represented. Who knows? It's just my opinion.

I do not want for this update to be sad. We have had a wonderful summer. For the most part, Nino has had more good days than bad. When we returned home today, we saw the doctor and now know that something definitely needs to be done about Nino's belly. We also believe that he will begin a new treatment when we return to NIH next week.

We are picking up Nino's birthday cake on Wednesday morning and then heading to the hospital at NIH. Nino has an afternoon appointment with Rehabilitation and Orthopedics, and then we can go back to The Inn for his cake and ice cream. Yeah! He has several appointments on Thursday, and then we will return home. I just wanted to let you know what our immediate plan was; I will keep you posted.

I do pray that the medications will not have a negative effect and that he will begin Kindergarten on August 30th. Believe me; I will have plenty of tissues on hand. After all, I cried every morning when I dropped him off at soccer camp this summer. Oh well, call me silly; but it is not easy!

There are a lot of great things going on in our lives. Thanks for being such a huge part of our journey. The book is ready to go. We only need a few more illustrations, and a decision needs to be made about publishing; and we're off. It is all too exciting! I hope we can make a difference. God has given us too many opportunities to see the light to not be able to share the message. Enjoy the last few weeks of summer. Take care of yourselves and each other. Give thanks for everything you experience, good or bad; and remember that it's the experience that makes us who we are.

Goodnight. God bless.

Love,

Lori

# Journal

8/20/04

Hello friends.

We arrived home around 6:00 tonight; but I couldn't begin to send an update until the Women's Gymnastics Olympic competition was over! Go USA!

The Tuesday before we left for NIH, we had a follow-up appointment with the GI doctor in Lancaster; do you pronounce it "Lan-cast-er" or "Lan-caster"? Anyway, the doctor decided to start a new stomach medication and hold off on making any decisions until we begin the new medications.

On Wednesday, we only had appointments with Rehabilitation and Orthopedics at NIH. They were able to build a cork insole into Nino's new sneakers, and it seems to make such a difference.

Nino's birthday celebration was great; there were so many Inn families who attended. His cake was terrific; everyone complimented about it. Thanks, Mr. Kilmore!

A family from Carlisle donated children's gifts to The Inn a few weeks ago, and they left a special package for Nino to open when he arrived. Thanks, Arp family!

# Journal

Today, we met with the Rheumatology team, who is pretty much running the whole program with the genetic studies. It was decided that Nino will begin a new immunosuppressant treatment. There are two drugs that we have been seriously discussing. Tony and I thought that we were going to choose Humira instead of Remicade; but after speaking with the gastroenterologist, the team at NIH, and the rheumatologist at Hershey, we have decided to try the Remicade. Unfortunately, Remicade is an infusion, which means that Nino will need to be in-patient for one day every four to six weeks. The doctors are suspecting that colitis is causing all of his stomach problems, and the Remicade has shown improvements in patients with colitis as well as with arthritis. Learning all of this, we have chosen the Remicade as the next step in our plan.

Unfortunately, there is a downside. We have learned that Remicade is just ANOTHER effective medication that is not approved for kids like Nino. Since our insurance will not cover the cost of the medication, Nino will need to get the infusions at NIH. Tony and I have no idea how we will work scheduling with the boys' school, sports, etc.; but we can, and we will! We have been traveling to NIH every six to seven weeks anyway; so it won't be *that big of a change. The first three treatments are done weekly, and then the routine will begin.*

*We are currently waiting for some results to come back from the gastroenterologist, and then we will know more concerning Nino's stomach situation. Also, next Tuesday, the doctor from NIH is supposed to contact me about the test results from today, as well as the approximate dates for starting the new treatments. We are nervous about the new treatments, but we know we are in great hands!*

*In addition, we were very pleased to hear that Nino's hearing test results were very good!*

*Again this visit to the Inn was humbling. It is such an honor to be a part of that family. We are the ones who are blessed. Our lives are so rich because of our experiences. Please keep in mind that the benefit for The Children's Inn is quickly approaching. It will be held on September 12th at the Boiling Springs Pool. We have a DJ, magician, tons of great prizes to be raffled off, hot dogs, burgers, and plans for lots of fun! Adults are $10, and kids are $5; remember, all proceeds go to The Children's Inn.*

*I am very nervous about Nino's beginning Kindergarten in a couple of weeks. I have been working with his teacher for a few months to help with* the transition. There are so many things to consider: Nino's exposure to germs, his seizures, his high fevers, his shyness, etc.; I was very comfortable and Nino was becoming comfortable. I just found out that there will be a new teacher, and I am devastated! There are a lot of new things that are happening with Nino all at one time, and I am very concerned about all of these changes happening at once. Please keep the prayers coming!

Well, the countdown is on; there are only a couple weeks left until the kids are back to school. Please try to enjoy the little bit of summer you have left. You know, I am going to miss my guys so much! I am very happy with our decision to send them back to Saint Patrick School; it is a wonderful learning place, but I am sad about missing so much time with them. I hope they remember all the life lessons they learned this past year. I pray they take nothing for granted. I want them to be strong and independent, yet sensitive and kind. I hope the biggest thing they are learning is compassion.

I should bring this to a close for tonight. I wanted to let you know how our visit went and what the new plan is. I know so many of you are anxious to hear. I cannot tell you what it means to us to have so much support from all of you!

May God continue to bless you and your families!

# Journal

Fondly,

Journal

Lori


8/25/04

Good Morning.

I have a confession to make. Each morning, while the boys are still in bed, I watch Joyce Meyers, a Christian Evangelist. It is a morning ritual that I've incorporated into my morning reflection time, and it has worked wonders for me. I was truly moved by what was on the show this morning, so I wanted to share my experience and what I learned with you.

Since our return from NIH, I have been a little worried and concerned about Nino's new treatments. My concern is not only for what is to come medically for him, but for how our family will handle everything. The timing will be more intense. The boys' schedules are full with school work, sports, friends, family, church, etc.; you know how it goes. We have been working with our NIH schedule since Thanksgiving; and we have been in a great routine that has worked for us. Now a new time begins. I am going back to those same feelings that I experienced when we first began Nino's journey; I am scared, but I have faith. I will not lie to you and tell you this is easy or that it has been easy; it has been very hard! This morning, I was moved to tears by Galatians 5:5. "But by faith we eagerly await through the righteousness for which we hope." Sounds pretty simple doesn't it? Think about it. Live by faith with guidance from the Spirit. Yeah, that is pretty simple. Joyce pointed out something very profound; she said that even when you are being "tested" that you must follow the Spirit and walk in faith, and do so more at those times than ever. If you live by the Spirit, you will walk by the Spirit. You see, the more I worry and doubt, the more my positive energy is drained. What good am I to anyone if I don't walk with the Spirit? Remember Father Hereshko talking with me about surrendering control? Yes, this is the big picture! Some of you are probably saying, "Here she goes again on one of those Bible rampages". We each make choices about how we will handle situations; I am choosing to trust in the Lord for guidance and support. He knows my heart better than anyone. He knows what the future holds; He is the light at the end of the tunnel. I am most thankful today for all of the blessings in my life. I realize how very fortunate I am.

Yesterday was the anniversary of my dad's death. Eleven years ago my father drowned in the Delaware River. Last night I asked Tony if he knew what day it was; and he of course remembered, and we talked about that day. Our lives will never be the same. It's hard to believe that so much time has passed and that so many things have been experienced and that he has not been here with us. I know he is in heaven watching over us and laughing at us too, especially with the four boys, you know! I often think about picking up the phone to call my mom. At the low times when I just want to cry or when I am feeling a little overwhelmed, I just want her to hug me. I'd love to have the opportunity to fight with her again about her smoking! I just have to keep focused on the times we had together and how rich I am for my parents' presence in my life.

Thanks for letting me share this message with you.

Dixie took the boys to get Nino's birthday gift and for a treat to McDonald's. I actually have a hair appointment, and I am really looking forward to it!

Make it a great day. Reach out and touch another heart today. You never know what a difference you will make in someone else's life.

God bless you and your families.

Love,

Lori

My enthusiasm for life has been strength for me. I embrace each day. I am glad I am able to do that. Someone recently said to me, "I admire how you never give up!" I was touched by that comment, but I was also a little puzzled. What choice do I have? My dad is dead! My son is sick! My mom is gone! What choice do I have? If I don't embrace each day, what message am I sending to my boys? What environment am I creating for my husband? What kind of friend would I be? More importantly, what kind of Christian would I be? Believing that I will see my parents again and knowing that God will take care of my son and our family, why would I not rejoice and celebrate each day?

# Journal

9/05/04

Hello Friends.

It is late Saturday evening, and this is the last update I will type that will be included in the book. This is so exciting, and I really wanted to share this with you. Look for the book in print some time in late December or in early January. The goal is to have the book published before Christmas. Next week the details will be finalized; and it's off to the publisher. This is a HUGE project!

This week has been crazy! I was so worried about Nino and his making the adjustment to school, but he is doing great! He loves school. Toward the end of the day, he begins to get pretty tired; but he doesn't let it stop him. He was running a fever a couple of days this week, and his legs were also a little sore; but he went to school and kept up with everyone else. I am so proud of him. I have not yet received word on the new schedule for his treatments, but I hope to hear sometime next week. I will definitely let you know.

Joe and Vinny also love school; they are so glad to be back at Saint Patrick School. It was so nice having them home last year and spending so much quality time together, but it is really nice listening to them tell about their day, and seeing their independence as well. Angelo is struggling, though! He wonders all day where "his boys" are. He must call their names a dozen times a day, and you should see his face light up when they come running to the car in car line.

Joey served 5:15 Mass tonight, and he is scheduled to serve noon Mass tomorrow. I took Joe by myself tonight; and tomorrow we will go as a family. The Gospel was wonderful. I felt as though it was meant for me. "If you do not carry your cross, you cannot come to me as my disciple." That is so true! We all have our cross to carry. We must continue to focus on the discipleship and do what needs to be done to reach that point.

In telling my story, I am trying to share what I have learned while carrying my cross and the way my relationship with God has intensified on this journey. I am no different than any of you. I am just choosing to reach out with my story and share how faith and hope have helped me to become stronger. I am so inspired when I talk to others. We learn so much from each other; we just have to listen with our hearts. We have to step out of our comfort zones and touch another life. I do not want to waste the time I have; I want to continue to learn and grow each day. I pray that sharing our journey with you has made you take a closer look at the gifts in your life.

# Journal

*Please mark your calendars for Sunday, September 12th! Please come out to the Boiling Springs Pool and help us give back to The Children's Inn.*

*The Children's Inn has made such an incredible difference in our lives. Adult tickets are $10, Children's tickets are $5, and Children under 2 are free.*

*A choice of a hot dog or burger lunch is included. Special features include a magician, face painting, and a DJ. A lot of gifts, including Allenbery Theatre tickets, will be raffled. I will tell our story and Courtney Wickard, a young girl from the area, will share her story and how The Inn has played a part in her life! Come out for a great cause and tons of fun! Tickets may be purchased at the pool that day, in addition to being purchased in advance.*

*So many people have been added to the mailing list due to people sending me an email or calling and saying, "Hey, please add my friend. Here is the address." I have been so touched by your reaching out to me. I am blown away by how many of you stop me and talk about the updates. If you do not wish to continue to receive updates, please send a quick email to let me know; and I will remove your email address.*

*Thank you for caring so much! We are stronger because of your belief in us and your prayers.*

# Journal

I want to bring this to a close by thanking you once again for being part of

this incredible journey.

I do not know what the future holds.

I am going to continue to reach out to others.

I am determined to make a difference.

I will continue to keep all of you in our prayers.

May God continue to bless you and your families.

Love,

Lori

At midnight on August 23, 1993, we received a call that would change our lives forever. I remember every moment; it was such a surreal feeling! The terror in Tony's eyes and the panicked way he instructed me to get the baby and grab some clothes alerted me to the seriousness of it all. We had to get to New Jersey! I knew for sure my mom had had a heart attack and was gone! I was so wrong! My dad had fallen off his boat in the middle of the Delaware River. It was assumed that he had drowned; his body was missing! I refused to believe that he was gone. I told everyone that he was out there somewhere in need of help. I knew he couldn't swim, nor would he have worn a life vest, since he had told me many times, "Wearing a life vest is a sign of weakness." I was in denial and terrified at the thought of never seeing my dad again. Although his body was missing for three days, I couldn't grasp the fact that he was gone!

At the time, I thought, why couldn't he have had cancer or some terminal illness? I would have had time to say goodbye. Can you imagine?

During this time, I prayed a lot! The days that his body was missing, I prayed that he'd be found alive. While we waited for the autopsy report, I prayed that he didn't suffer. The day of his memorial service, I prayed for strength. Finally, I just prayed for peace! *Looking back now I see that time in my life very differently; I see it as a time of preparation!*

Over the next few years our lives were drastically changed. We learned that we were expecting. Initially, our physician informed us that I was carrying twins; we were so excited! During an ultrasound at eighteen weeks, it was discovered that only one twin had a heartbeat. Again, I had another blow; and I turned to prayer for comfort. Months later when we welcomed our second son, Vinny, into our lives, we were overwhelmed with happiness! Being an only child, and experiencing the loss of my dad, I didn't want our son Joey to grow up without siblings. What I experienced as an only child were wonderful times, but they were also lonely times. I wanted more for Joey; a sibling would give him the connection that I missed. The day Joey met his baby brother at the hospital the peace I felt in my heart was overwhelming!

A year later we moved to a new area, which was a new adventure! Not a day went by that I didn't think about my dad. Routinely I traveled back and forth from Pennsylvania to New Jersey to care for my mom. She was having a lot of health problems and was in and out of the hospital often. My husband was keeping busy with work and loving his new assignment. The boys were growing so quickly. Vinny was in Pre-Kindergarten, and Joe was in Kindergarten. They were playing sports and making many great friends. I loved being a mom and also took a part-time job coaching gymnastics. I was having the time of my life!

A new son, Nino, graced us with his presence a couple of years later. We now had three sons. Wow! My mom decided to move to our area to be closer to the boys; they were everything to her! Life was really good; but I still missed my dad terribly.

Nino added so much joy to our lives. I cannot describe how important it was to me to have three sons. What amazing gifts we were given! All I have ever wanted to be was a wife and mother; all my dreams were now a reality.

There were many hospital visits for my mom during this time. She struggled daily with her health, and she never fully recovered from the loss of my dad. When she was well, she spent all of her time with the boys. They went to the park, played with squirt guns, played with bubble wands, read stories, completed art projects, etc… When Mom was sick, it was their turn to take care of her. They would read to her, sing to her, draw for her, or just hang out and watch silly shows on television together. Oh my how I cherish those memories now!

As time progressed, there were many signs that Nino wasn't well. He had horrible reflux, cried all the time, and seemed so uncomfortable. Each time I questioned the doctor about his symptoms, I was told that I was overreacting. I never should have second guessed my motherly instincts. I should have trusted my judgment. I am his mom, and it is up to me to take care of him! Oh the things I've learned!

At the time of his first surgery there were suspicions of Leukemia or Lymphoma. We didn't understand how this could be happening. This was our baby. How was this even possible? My conversations with God were full of questions and blame: *Isn't it bad enough that You took my dad from me? How about all my poor mom is going through? How much more can You do to me?* I was very bitter! I began analyzing everything to death; I thought there had to be a hidden agenda behind everything.

When Nino's biopsy results were benign, we rejoiced. What an experience! Imagine facing the ocean and someone yelling to you to jump to the other side. The good news we received gave us the strength to take that jump and land safely on the other side. Several months later Nino experienced his first of many flares. Little did we know what was to come.

I remember praying the same words that I prayed when my dad died. I asked God *to keep me strong; I asked for understanding and wisdom. I prayed for His guidance above all else.* This was a very difficult time for all of us. For months flares which involved high fevers, rash, joint pain, and febrile seizures were happening regularly. We felt so helpless. I stopped praying as often as I had been. I guess I was blaming God a little bit. I thought maybe He could have spread the tragedies around to others instead of dumping them all on me. I was feeling a little sorry for myself.

How was I supposed to handle all of this? I continued to question

my relationship with God. I also began to question my relationship

with my husband. I thought that I could handle everything on my

own. I really didn't think I needed anyone except my boys. I was

determined to help Nino, take care of my mom, raise my boys, and

do it alone! What was I thinking? I did a lot of soul searching and

realized how unhappy and scared I was. I made a commitment to

give my heart to the Lord and to open my heart to the others in my

life. When I made a re-commitment to my husband, I felt that no

two people on earth could experience the bond between us.

We both have that never ending, unconditional love for our boys,

which strengthens our love and commitment for one another. We

both agreed that whatever happens, we are in "this" for life! We

also didn't know where our journey would take us; but we knew

with God on our side, we could handle anything!

My mom continued to have serious health problems and many

hospital stays. In July of 2001, my mom had a serious scare and

was on a ventilator for weeks. I basically lived at the hospital while

Tony, for the most part, stayed home and took care of the house and the boys.

One day after Tony and I met with the doctors and our priest, we made the decision to stop all life support. Later that evening Tony and I sat with my mom and said our goodbyes. How thankful I am now for the opportunity to say goodbye to my mom, since I felt I was cheated of that opportunity with my dad. My mom was able to communicate sometimes, and she expressed herself beautifully to me. She said, "Goodbye," and told me that she was ready to be with my dad! I shared with her what an amazing gift I felt she was in our lives, and I expressed how very much I loved her!

The next morning while Tony and I were at her side, the doctors turned off the ventilator. By afternoon, she was breathing on her own. It wasn't her time yet! My mom was never the same person again. Her fight, her fire, was gone. She was still functioning, but her heart was not soft. She lost her compassion and her desire for life. Externally she was going through the motions, but internally she was empty. Many physical ailments were causing this change in her, but the greater reason was that she had given up. The night we said goodbye, it really was goodbye. The mom I knew was no longer there; she was just a shell of the woman I called "Mom".

Not even a year later we welcomed our fourth son Angelo. Our family was now complete! I thought having three sons was wonderful, but it was truly amazing to have four. It was so cool! Nino had many months of minimal pain because he was taking an anti-inflammatory medication that was working very well, or so we thought. One early morning in April, he woke up screaming with belly pain, and ulcers were discovered. From that point on, he got sicker by the day. By September, there was talk of starting a chemotherapeutic treatment. *This is our four-year-old son. What were they telling us?*

Tony and I prayed for a miracle. It was very hard, but we knew we had to put our faith to the test. We had to remember that it is not our will, but His will that would be done. Those days were tough! In November of 2003, many prayers were answered when our journey took us to National Institutes of Health in Bethesda, Maryland. This would be the saving grace for our son and our family.

For the most part my mom was doing well. She was helping

as much as she could with the boys, and it was so nice having

her around. She did spend a lot of time doing projects with the

boys while we were home schooling. Things were really coming

together.

Tony accepted a new position. He was very excited about it, and

we were very proud of him. Nino was getting sicker, but we were

trying to keep our family life as normal as possible. Life went on

as best as it could. I was actually missing my dad now more than

ever. Ten years had passed since his death, and I still cried each

time I thought of him.

As our journeys to NIH continued, my mom stayed with the other

boys and did home schooling with them while Tony and I took

Nino to the hospital.

Just before our third visit to NIH, another call would forever

change our lives. My mom was gone! She died in her sleep. She

died peacefully. I again turned to prayer. I talked to God. I thanked

Him. I thanked Him for letting her go to be with my dad. I thanked

Him for all the extra time He lent her to us. I thanked Him for the peace in my heart!

I believe the Lord is present in every situation; you just have to look for Him.

Our journey continues, moment to moment.

Tony and I are doing all we can for Nino and for our boys.

Experiences shape who you are. *"Who you are is God's gift to you. What you make of yourself is your gift back to God!"* We call these experiences our journey. We don't know where this path will take us. We only know where we've been, and what we've learned along the way.

Each of us is on our own journey. Many of us experience situations in life that we never could have imagined. With the grace of God and some determination, we get through.

Our journey goes on. We will live life moment by moment, and will continue to cherish every single memory!

Nothing is forever, except God's love.

Embrace His love, and embark upon your journey!

Nino is committed to a protocol at NIH until he is eighteen years old.

Hopefully with the information the doctors learn from Nino, other children and families will be helped and/or healed.

The updates continue.

Our journey goes on.

For now, we will live life moment by moment.

We will continue to cherish every single memory!

I can see water for miles. It is really all I can see.

Each time I think I will never reach the other side, I take the

jump and feel the land beneath my feet!

With grateful hearts to all of you…


Medical Professionals

Family

Friends

Community

~ Lori


Thank you to my son for giving me inspiration, to my bosses

for giving me time to illustrate, to my parents for giving me

encouragement, and to God for giving me my talent.

~ Gary

# About the Author

Lori Todaro is a wife and mother of four sons. She was also the only child of two amazing parents. Through adversity she has developed into a confident woman of faith who believes there is good in every situation. Experiencing the drowning death of her father, her Mother's long illness and death, and taking care of her son who has a chronic illness, Lori has become determined to reach out to others. In her journal entries she tells how she manages to stay strong and believe the best no matter what challenges she faces. Lori hopes her story will encourage others to always be their very best and to go the extra mile for someone else. Above all, to never take anything for granted. She is honored to share her personal story and hopes to touch a life.

CPSIA information can be obtained
at www.ICGtesting.com
Printed in the USA
BVHW03s1117160318
510514BV00003B/39/P

9 781420 811056